ACPL ITEM

DISCARDED

SO-DSF-910

MAY 5 '67

THE *'I Love Garlic'* COOKBOOK

COOKBOOKS BY WILLIAM I. KAUFMAN

THE ART OF CREOLE COOKERY

THE ART OF INDIA'S COOKERY

THE COFFEE COOKBOOK

THE NUT COOKBOOK

THE 'I LOVE PEANUT BUTTER' COOKBOOK

THE HOT DOG COOKBOOK

THE TEA COOKBOOK

THE CATHOLIC COOKBOOK

COOKING IN A CASTLE

THE WONDERFUL WORLD OF COOKING SERIES

THE STAND-UP COOKBOOK SERIES

THE ART OF CASSEROLE COOKERY

THE SUGAR FREE COOKBOOK

THE SUGAR FREE COOKBOOK OF FAMILY
FAVORITES

THE APPLE COOKBOOK

THE
'I Love Garlic'
COOKBOOK

William I. Kaufman

Garden City, New York

DOUBLEDAY & COMPANY, INC.

1967

Library of Congress Catalog Card Number 67–11173

Copyright © 1967 by William I. Kaufman
All Rights Reserved

Printed in the United States of America
First Edition

THE 'I LOVE GARLIC' COOKBOOK
is dedicated to
a lover of fine food
my dear fan, Henri Lauga

1394686

Contents

Recipes for items printed in small capital letters can be found by consulting the Index.

A SHORT HISTORY OF GARLIC AND HINTS AS TO ITS USAGE

If one could set a lyric to a garlic lover's song, I think that it might start out something like "Oh, the smell of it, Oh, the taste of it, Oh, the savor of garlic."

Garlic is a member of the lily family and is closely allied to the onion. The root is a compound bulb with several small sections of cloves held together by a common membrane. It has been under cultivation for many centuries and is native to Siberia. Its English name is derived from the Anglo-Saxon "garleac"—"gar" meaning spear and "leac" meaning leek—words which describe its appearance as it grows with its bulbous root and its tassel of green, spearlike leaves.

In ancient China garlic was used as one of the magical potions to ward off the evil eye. In India it was a favorite for centuries for improving the voice, intellect, and complexion. In early Sanskrit, the ancient tongue of India, one of its names is "slayer of monsters." Egyptians early utilized garlic as a cooking herb and the Israelites, trudging hungrily in the wilderness after their flight from bondage, reported their yearning for the delicacies of that land: "We remember the fish, which we did eat in Egypt freely; the cucumbers, and the melons, and the leeks, and the onions, and the garlic" (Numbers 11:5). The classical Greeks were unimpressed by garlic but Homer mentions it as does Herodotus, while the Romans, who disliked the strong flavor of garlic, nevertheless believed it to have magical powers. They fed it to their soldiers to make them courageous, and to their laborers to give them strength. Medicinal claims have been made for garlic since ancient days. Pliny claimed it to be the remedy for sixty-one ailments and even Aristotle lauded its curative powers in his writings. Chaucer, in his *Canterbury Tales,* takes up the thread of the trinity of flavoring mentioned by the Israelites. One tale reveals that among the pilgrims there was one who relished garlic, onions, and leeks. The family relationship of the three vegetables has long been known. In Elizabethan England Thomas Nashe, an early satirist, alluded to the long-held belief of people in the cold countries that garlic encouraged drunkenness when he tersely wrote, "Garlick maketh a man wynke, drynke, and stynke."

Despite the disdainful sniffs from the northlanders, the judicious use of garlic became one of the marks of gourmet cookery in China, India, and in the lands bordering the Mediterranean. Spanish and Portuguese explorers carried it with them to the New World where it readily combined with the vast panoply of native herbs used by the Mayans and the Aztecs. Today, garlic is indispensable to Latin-American cooking.

The early colonists brought with them their derogatory opinion of this special herb when they came to the New World, although in fairness they acknowledged its excellence when used by the French. Under these conditions it wasn't until the middle of the nineteenth century that an influx of garlic-loving immigrants changed the culinary climate and started the trend which has given garlic its great popularity on our shores. The French, Italians, Greeks, Slavs, and Middle Easterners brought the love of the herb to our eastern coast while the Chinese and others of the Orient brought it to the west. Mexicans who crossed the borders of the Southwest added to its increasing use.

A Moslem legend tells that when Satan left the Garden of Eden in triumph after Adam's fall, onions sprang up in his right footprint and garlic in his left. And so we must give the devil his due. Today, garlic leaves its own important imprint. All over America chefs, housewives, and outdoor barbecue artists flavor meats, vegetables, soups, tomato dishes, salads, pickles, and relishes with fresh or instant forms of this perennial plant with the bulbous root. Some of the world's most tempting dishes have the "now you smell it, now you don't" fragrance of this potent cousin of the lily.

Even though fresh garlic predominates in the recipes of THE 'I LOVE GARLIC' COOKBOOK, the reader has the choice of using garlic salt or garlic powder should she so desire. Anyone who is in a hurry; anyone who has no fresh garlic on hand, may simply consult the table of substitutions in the front of this book.

Garlic is so available in our supermarkets and specialty food stores that it is not necessary for us to stock a large supply. The shopper may pick up a box or a bag that contains as few as two or three bulbs of this flavorsome herb without the fear of its being in short supply when more is needed. Garlic is plentiful throughout the year. It is cured in the fields, packed in net bags, and then stored under refrigeration with a relatively high humidity. To avoid the loss of its water content, practical housewives preserve their garlic in the refrigerator, although it is certainly attractive to see strings of garlic bulbs hanging in a kitchen. Many true garlic lovers keep such strings of garlic hanging near their work space in readiness, as it is not uncommon for them to use several bulbs per week in the creation of their culinary specialties. For those who use garlic occasionally, storage in the refrigerator is recommended as being the best way to keep the bulbs from shrinking and becoming unusable.

One of the most wonderful things about garlic is that each clove can be separated easily from its bulb without the entire bulb having to be cut. Consequently there is no escape of odor from the garlic until it is in use; its flavor stays locked in by nature.

Because the juice of the garlic has such potency I recommend that a small cutting board be set aside for the sole use of chopping or mincing garlic. In this way one avoids having the garlic oils mingle with other foods which may need dicing.

By breaking a clove of garlic from the bulb and holding it with a fork or a piece of waxed paper, one can peel it and cut away the thin tissues of the garlic without touching it. Minced or chopped garlic or garlic that has been put through a very handy gadget called a garlic press will easily brown and practically dissolve in most cooking mixtures. Crushed, minced, or chopped, garlic is excellent in sauces and gravies, as well as main dishes, and should be used frequently. When whole cloves are used in these preparations, remember to strain the juices before serving.

Tissue-thin slivers of garlic, crushed with salt, pepper, and other seasoning, add zest to any dish made with tomatoes and of course these same kinds of slivers slipped under the skin of roasts of lamb, beef, and pork will result in meats with magnificent flavor. The piquancy of chops and steaks is improved by rubbing them with a cut clove of garlic before broiling. Small turkeys and broiler-fryers increase their tastiness and tenderness if they are rubbed with a cut clove of garlic that has been combined with a little cooking oil and if they are permitted to stand an hour or so at room temperature before cooking. Those who may be hesitant to use garlic and fearful of adding too much too soon have two alternatives. One way is to start out by using a very small amount of crushed garlic, increasing the amount until one gets to exactly the point that suits the taste. The other way is to use instant or powdered garlic, measuring it off very carefully starting with a quarter teaspoon and increasing the measurement until the flavor pleases the palate.

I love garlic and I am confident that as the proud possessor of THE 'I LOVE GARLIC' COOKBOOK you will agree with the philosophy of the great Louis Diat, famous French chef of another era, who said, "Garlic is the fifth element of living and as important to our existence as earth, air, fire, and water."

No matter whether you crush it, mince it, chop it, dice it, rub it, sprinkle it, brush it, or spread it, you show your true colors as a garlic lover when, in any form, wherever or whenever possible, you use garlic.

And so ends this hymn of praise to a daring herb—"Oh, the taste of it, Oh, the smell of it, fills my heart and palate with joy!"

In THE 'I LOVE GARLIC' COOKBOOK a large variety of recipes in every category is offered to permit all American cooks to put into their pots and salad bowls the subtle "magic" that comes from the judicious use of garlic—the magic that makes the diner's mouth water and gives the hostess a reputation for sheer culinary genius. Everybody will say I LOVE GARLIC!!

WILLIAM I. KAUFMAN

AUTHOR'S NOTE

I am including here an exchange table for those who are in a hurry or those who do not have fresh garlic on hand.

Instant minced garlic when reconstituted has the same volume as an equal amount of fresh garlic.

½ medium-size clove garlic = $\frac{1}{16}$ teaspoon instant garlic powder

1 medium-size clove garlic = $\frac{1}{8}$ teaspoon instant garlic powder

2 medium-size cloves garlic = $\frac{1}{4}$ teaspoon instant garlic powder

At the present time the smallest spoon of a set of measuring spoons holds ¼ teaspoon. To measure ⅛ teaspoon of instant garlic powder, for example, fill and level the ¼ teaspoon measure. Cut away and return to the jar an even half. To measure $\frac{1}{16}$ of instant garlic powder, you would fill and level the same ¼ teaspoon measure, then cut away half and half again. This amount would be equal to what the French chefs call a "point" of garlic. We call it a "pinch."

Appetizers

A clove of garlic worn in the buttonhole of the
bridegroom insures a successful wedding night.

—Ancient Palestinian superstition

ROQUEFORT CHEESE SPREAD

½ cup finely crumbled
  Roquefort cheese
½ cup creamy cottage
  cheese
¼ cup sour cream
¼ teaspoon dried
  crumbled dill seed
½ teaspoon whole savory
  leaves, crumbled

1 teaspoon crumbled
  whole tarragon leaves
⅛ teaspooon ground
  white pepper
⅛ teaspoon onion
  powder
½ clove garlic, crushed

Combine all ingredients. Mix until thoroughly blended.

Yield: Approximately 1 cup.

HOT CHILI ROQUEFORT CANAPES

4 ounces cream cheese
2 tablespoons (1½
  ounces) crumbled
  Roquefort cheese
1 tablespoon ketchup

1¾ teaspoons chili powder
¼ teaspoon paprika
½ clove garlic, crushed
10 slices of bread

Soften cream cheese and blend with Roquefort cheese. Add
ketchup and spices and mix well.

Trim crust from bread and toast on both sides. Spread
with cheese mixture and cut each piece into 3 strips.

Place on baking sheets. Broil until browned and bubbly.
Garnish with paprika.

Yield: 30 canapés.

CANAPES A LA CREOLE

½ cup finely chopped
onion
2 cloves garlic, minced
1 tablespoon butter or
margarine
1 cup finely chopped
boiled or cooked ham
¾ cup finely chopped
fresh tomatoes

½ cup finely chopped
raw green pepper
½ teaspoon salt
¼ teaspoon ground
black pepper
¼ teaspoon chili powder
1⁄16 teaspoon cayenne
8 slices bread
Grated Parmesan cheese
Parsley flakes

Sauté onion and garlic 2 to 3 minutes in butter or margarine along with ham. Add tomatoes, green pepper, salt, and spices. Cook and stir until mixture is dry. Set aside.

Trim crust from bread; cut each slice into 4 strips. Arrange on baking sheets. Place under broiler, turning to toast bread on both sides.

Spread the creole mixture on one side of each strip of bread. Sprinkle generously with grated Parmesan cheese. Bake in a 350°F. oven 5 minutes. Serve hot garnished with parsley flakes. *Yield:* 32 canapés.

ANCHOVY ABBADABBAS

1 cup sifted all-purpose
flour
½ teaspoon salt
¾ teaspoon powdered
mustard
1⁄16 teaspoon cayenne
2 cloves garlic, crushed

⅓ cup butter or
margarine
3 tablespoons cold water
2 tablespoons butter or
margarine, melted
Anchovy paste
¼ cup grated Cheddar
cheese

Sift together first 4 ingredients. Add garlic and butter or margarine and cut it in with pastry blender or two knives until mixture is the consistency of coarse meal. Sprinkle in cold water. Mix only to form a dough. Chill 2 hours, or until dough is firm enough to roll.

Roll into two 9×7×⅛-inch rectangles on a lightly floured board. Brush melted butter or margarine over top. Spread thinly with anchovy paste and sprinkle with grated cheese. Roll up in jelly-roll fashion. Wrap in waxed paper and chill until firm enough to slice.

Cut into slices ¼ inch thick. Place on lightly greased baking sheets. Bake in a 400°F. oven 12 to 14 minutes, or until lightly browned. Serve as a canapé or with salads.

Yield: 36.

CURRIED BEEF PATTIES

½ cup finely chopped onion	1½ teaspoons salt
2 tablespoons butter or margarine	¼ teaspoon ground black pepper
½ pound ground lean chuck	4 cloves garlic, crushed
½ cup finely chopped fresh tomato	1 teaspoon curry powder
	1 egg, slightly beaten
	Pastry
	1 egg white

Sauté onion in butter or margarine 1 to 2 minutes. Add ground chuck and stir and cook until meat turns gray. Add tomato, salt, black pepper, garlic, and curry powder. Cook 5 minutes, or until tomato is done.

Remove from heat and gradually stir in beaten egg. Stir and cook over low heat 1 minute to thicken the mixture. Cool.

Roll pastry out to ⅛-inch thickness. Cut into rounds with a 2½-inch pastry cutter. Spread 1 teaspoon meat filling on half of each circle of pastry. Fold the remaining half of the pastry over the meat in half-moon fashion. Press and crimp edges together with a fork. Prick top of each. Brush tops with egg white beaten until slightly foamy. Bake in a 450°F. oven 12 minutes, or until browned around the edges.

Yield: Approximately 30 patties.

SHAD ROE PATE

½ teaspoon salt
2 shad roe (¾ pound)
1 cup boiling water
1 tablespoon butter or margarine
1 tablespoon flour
½ cup light cream or top milk
½ teaspoon celery seed
½ teaspoon chervil leaves
½ teaspoon marjoram leaves
½ teaspoon tarragon leaves
¼ teaspoon basil leaves
2 cloves garlic, crushed
⅛ teaspoon cayenne
1½ teaspoons salt
2 teaspoons instant minced onion
5 teaspoons fresh lemon juice
18 slices bread or 72 crackers
Pimiento

Add salt and shad roe to boiling water, cover, and simmer 15 minutes. Remove from water, drain well, and mash.

Melt butter or margarine in a saucepan. Blend in flour. Stir in cream or top milk. Cook until of medium thickness, stirring constantly. Add seasonings, lemon juice, and mashed shad roe. Mix well. Chill until ready to serve.

Trim crust from bread and toast both sides. Spread with shad roe pâté. Cut each slice into 4 squares. Or serve pâté on crackers. Garnish with pimiento strips as desired.

Yield: 72.

MEAT PATTIES

½ cup fine, soft bread
   crumbs
⅓ cup milk
1 egg, beaten
1 pound ground chuck
1 cup ground ham
½ cup finely chopped
   onion
2 tablespoons minced
   green pepper

1½ teaspoons salt
1 teaspoon oregano
   leaves
½ teaspoon ground black
   pepper
2 cloves garlic, minced
¼ teaspoon ground
   allspice

Soak bread crumbs in milk. Mix with remaining ingredients.

Shape into 1-inch patties or balls. Arrange meat on the broiler rack and broil 10 minutes, or until browned, turning to brown on all sides. Serve as a hot hors d'oeuvre.

Yield: 45 to 50 small cocktail balls.

DINNER-SIZE PATTIES:

Shape mixture into 5 patties. Cook over the charcoal grill or broil in oven or in skillet over medium heat.

Yield: 5 servings.

CURRIED CHICKEN-LIVER TURNOVERS

PASTRY:

¼ pound butter or margarine
1 3-ounce package cream cheese
1 cup sifted all-purpose flour

With fingers, work butter or margarine and cream cheese into sifted flour. When well blended, form into roll, wrap in waxed paper, and chill several hours or overnight.

Roll very thin. Cut into 2-inch circles. Place a teaspoon of the filling on each round. Fold over and seal. Bake in a 400°F. oven until brown, about 5 to 8 minutes. Sprinkle lightly with salt and curry powder. Serve as a hot hors d'oeuvre.

FILLING:

*½ cup boiled chicken
  livers
2 hard-cooked eggs
1 teaspoon grated onion
¼ teaspoon salt
⅛ teaspoon ground black
  pepper*

*1 teaspoon curry powder
Dash ginger
Dash garlic powder
3 to 4 tablespoons heavy
  cream*

Combine livers and eggs. Chop very fine or press through fine sieve. Add remaining ingredients, using just enough cream to moisten.

Yield: 30.

PICKLED SALMON

*1 pound salmon steaks
3 to 4 tablespoons butter
  or margarine
1 cup cider vinegar
1½ tablespoons sweet
  pepper flakes
½ cup finely chopped
  onion*

*½ teaspoon whole allspice
2 teaspoons sugar
1½ teaspoons salt
1 clove garlic, crushed
1 hot red pepper (1½
  inches long)*

Cut salmon into 1-inch squares. Sauté in butter or margarine. Place in a flat casserole.

In a small saucepan, combine vinegar, sweet pepper flakes, onion, allspice, sugar, salt, and garlic. Break red pepper in half and add. Bring to boiling point and boil 1 minute. Pour over fish.

Marinate at least 24 hours before serving, turning fish from time to time to marinate uniformly. Serve on toothpicks as appetizer or on rounds of toast.

Yield: Approximately 30 pieces.

CEYLON CURRY PUFFS

¼ *cup finely chopped raw pork*
¼ *cup finely chopped raw lamb*
½ *cup finely chopped raw chicken*
1 slice raw bacon, finely chopped
2 tablespoons butter or margarine
½ *cup finely chopped onion*
1 clove garlic, crushed
¼ *teaspoon ground cinnamon*

¼ *teaspoon ground ginger*
¼ *teaspoon ground cayenne*
2 teaspoons ground coriander
Small pinch whole saffron
¼ *cup chopped fresh tomato*
1¼ *teaspoons salt*
¼ *cup milk*
⅓ *cup finely chopped cooked potatoes*
1 hard-cooked egg, finely chopped
CEYLON PASTRY
1 egg white, slightly beaten

Combine meats and set aside.

Melt butter or margarine in a saucepan and brown lightly. Sauté onion in browned butter or margarine 1 minute. Add spices and cook 1 minute. Add tomato, meat, and salt. Cook 2 to 3 minutes. Stir in milk and cook until liquid is almost absorbed. Add potatoes and egg. Turn out onto plate to cool.

Roll pastry paper thin on lightly floured board. Cut into circles with a 2½-inch cookie cutter. Brush edges with slightly beaten egg white. Place a rounded ½ teaspoon of the curry mixture in the center of each. Fold over the dough and crimp edges with a fork, being sure they are well sealed. Fry in hot deep fat (360°F. to 375°F.) until golden brown. Drain on absorbent paper. Serve as an accompaniment to cocktails or tomato juice.

Yield: 60.

CEYLON PASTRY:

2 cups sifted all-purpose
  flour
½ teaspoon salt
½ teaspoon double-acting
  baking powder

¼ cup butter or
  margarine
1 egg yolk, beaten
¼ cup milk

Sift the first 3 ingredients together into a mixing bowl. Cut in butter or margarine. Beat egg yolk with milk and add to make a stiff dough.

MARINATED FISH

1 pound fillet of haddock
  or other fish
3 tablespoons butter or
  margarine
1 cup cider vinegar
1 tablespoon sweet
  pepper flakes

½ cup finely chopped
  onion
½ teaspoon whole allspice
1½ teaspoons salt
1 clove garlic, crushed
1 hot red pepper, 1½
  inches long (broken in
  half)

Rinse fish and cut into 1½-inch squares. Sauté in butter or margarine. Place in a flat casserole.

In a small saucepan combine remaining ingredients. Bring to boiling point and boil 1 minute. Pour over fish. Marinate at least 24 hours before serving, turning fish from time to time.

Serve as an entree, for breakfast, or as an hors d'oeuvre.

Yield: 42 to 48 hors d'oeuvre.

SPICED KEBABS

1 pound lamb, cut into ¾-inch cubes
¼ pound lamb suet, finely chopped
¼ cup finely chopped onion
½ teaspoon ground cumin seed
1½ teaspoons paprika
1½ teaspoons dried parsley flakes
1 teaspoon ground coriander
1 clove garlic, crushed
½ small bay leaf
¾ teaspoon salt
⅛ teaspoon ground black pepper
3 tablespoons olive or salad oil

Combine all ingredients in a mixing bowl. Let stand 3 to 4 hours, preferably in refrigerator, for meat to absorb flavor of spices.

Arrange on skewers and broil over charcoal or in oven broiler 5 minutes, or until kebabs are brown and crisp on all sides. Serve on toothpicks with cocktails.

Yield: 40 kebabs.

NOTE: For main course, cut meat into 1½-inch cubes. Broil until browned.

CHILLED CAULIFLOWER LEMONETTE

2 10-ounce packages
frozen cauliflower or 2
small heads fresh
cauliflower
1 teaspoon grated lemon
peel
3 tablespoons fresh lemon
juice
½ cup olive or salad oil

½ teaspoon salt
⅛ teaspoon pepper
¼ teaspoon crumbled
oregano
3 tablespoons chopped
green pepper
2 tablespoons chopped
canned pimiento
1 clove garlic, crushed

Cut cauliflower into medium-size flowerets. Cook in 1 inch boiling, salted water 3 to 5 minutes, or until crispy-tender but not soft. Drain and cool.

Combine remaining ingredients in a bowl, blending well; add cauliflower and marinate for several hours at room temperature. Remove garlic.

Serve as appetizer, relish, or meat accompaniment.

Yield: 6 to 8 servings.

CLAM CANAPES

⅓ cup cottage cheese
1 3-ounce package cream
cheese
2 teaspoons fresh lemon
juice
½ teaspoon salt

½ teaspoon ground thyme
1 clove garlic, crushed
1/16 teaspoon cayenne
¾ pound clams
12 slices bread
Paprika

Combine cottage cheese, cream cheese, lemon juice, salt, and spices.

Remove clams from shells by running a knife around the

edge. Put clams through a food chopper, using the medium blade. Blend with the cream cheese mixture. Trim crust from bread slices and cut each slice into 4 squares. Spread with clam mixture. Sprinkle paprika over the tops. Broil until bubbly and hot. Serve hot as a cocktail accompaniment.

Yield: 48 canapés.

HOT-HOT SAUCE

1 tablespoon olive or
salad oil
1 large onion, chopped
2 cups chopped fresh
tomatoes
¼ cup tomato paste
½ cup water
2 tablespoons sweet
pepper flakes

1 bay leaf
2 teaspoons sugar
½ teaspoon oregano
leaves, crushed
¼ teaspoon crushed red
pepper
1½ teaspoons chili powder
1 clove garlic, crushed

Heat olive or salad oil in a 1½-quart saucepan. Add onion and cook over low heat 10 minutes, or until golden. Stir in chopped tomatoes, tomato paste, water, sweet pepper flakes, bay leaf, sugar, oregano, and crushed red pepper. Cover and cook 15 minutes, or until thickened. Stir in chili powder and garlic and simmer for 5 minutes. Remove from heat.

Serve hot or cold as a dip with corn chips or sturdy potato chips.

Yield: 1½ cups.

HERBED CLAM DIP

1 3-ounce package cream
cheese
¼ cup sour cream
1 tablespoon fresh lemon
juice
¼ cup minced canned
clams, well drained
1 teaspoon salt

¼ teaspoon ground basil
2 tablespoons minced
onion
2 cloves garlic, crushed
Dash ground black
pepper
Dash cayenne
Crisp celery hearts

Blend together cream cheese and sour cream. Add lemon juice, clams, salt, basil, onion, garlic, black pepper, and cayenne. Beat until fluffy.

Serve in a bowl on a large plate surrounded with celery hearts.

Yield: Approximately ¾ cup.

GARLIC CHEESE DIP

½ cup (¼ pound)
crumbled Roquefort
cheese
1 8-ounce package cream
cheese
¼ cup sweet cream or
milk

¼ cup finely chopped
red onion
4 cloves garlic, crushed
1 tablespoon fresh lemon
juice
Paprika

Mix Roquefort cheese with cream cheese and cream or milk until smooth. Add onion, garlic, and lemon juice and mix well.

Serve as a dip for potato chips, crackers, or vegetable

sticks. Garnish with paprika. The consistency of this dip is such that it may be used as a canapé spread.

Yield: A generous 1⅓ cups.

SOUR CREAM DIP

½ cup sour cream
¼ cup minced canned
clams, well drained
2 cloves garlic, crushed
2 tablespoons minced
onion
Dash cayenne

Dash ground black
pepper
¼ teaspoon basil leaves,
crumbled
¼ teaspoon salt
Paprika

Combine first 8 ingredients. Mix well.

Serve, garnished with paprika, in a small attractive bowl placed on a large hors d'oeuvre tray surrounded with carrot and celery sticks, raw cauliflower and raw broccoli flowerets, radish roses, potato chips, and small crackers.

Yield: ¾ cup.

GARLIC BREAD

½ cup butter or margarine
2 cloves garlic, crushed
Long loaf French bread

Melt butter or margarine in a saucepan. Add garlic and set aside.

Cut French bread diagonally into thick slices, almost to the bottom. Pour garlic butter generously between slices and over top of bread. Wrap in aluminum foil. Bake in a 375°F. oven 15 minutes, or until hot. *Yield:* 6 servings.

PIZZA

DOUGH:

1 yeast cake
1 teaspoon sugar
2 tablespoons lukewarm
    water
2 cups scalded milk,
    cooled to lukewarm

6 cups sifted all-purpose
    flour
½ cup peanut oil
1 teaspoon salt
⅓ cup cornmeal

FILLING:

3½ cups drained tomatoes
2 teaspoons salt
1 clove garlic, crushed
½ teaspoon oregano
1 teaspoon thyme

1 cup grated Parmesan
    or Romano cheese
¾ pound Italian sausage
2 tablespoons peanut oil

For dough, crumble yeast with a fork. Add sugar and water and mix until yeast is liquid. Add milk and 2 cups of the flour. Beat until smooth. Cover and let stand in a warm place until light and double in bulk, about 1 hour. Then add peanut oil, salt, and remainder of flour (about 4 cups) and mix together thoroughly. Toss out onto well-floured board and knead about 10 minutes until smooth and satiny. Place in bowl and again let rise until double in bulk. Divide dough and press with oiled fingers into baking sheets which have been sprinkled with cornmeal. Turn up outside edges to hold sauce.

For filling, mix together first 5 ingredients and spread out evenly over dough. Sprinkle the tomato mixture with grated cheese, crumbled sausage, and peanut oil. Bake in a 425°F. oven 20 to 25 minutes, or until dough is lightly browned. Serve hot, cut in several servings as appetizer, or serve as an accompaniment to beverages between meals.

Variation: After pizza filling has been added, top half of pizza with ¼ cup canned sliced mushrooms and other half with ½ cup shredded Cheddar cheese and a few anchovy fillets.

Yield: two 17×11-inch pies.

Soups

We remember the fish, which we did eat in Egypt freely; the cucumbers, and the melons, and the leeks, and the onions, and the garlic.

—*Numbers 11:5*

GARLIC SOUP

3 large tomatoes, peeled
2 cups water
5 cloves garlic, crushed
½ teaspoon paprika
½ teaspoon salt

2 tablespoons olive oil
2 green peppers, sliced
2 slices French or Italian
   bread, cut in half

Cook tomatoes in the water.
Blend together in bowl or mortar the garlic, paprika, salt, and oil. Place tomatoes, hot tomato liquid, peppers, and garlic mixture in blender. Blend on high speed until puréed. Place half slice of bread in bottom of each of 4 soup dishes. Pour garlic soup over.

Yield: 4 servings.   1394686

GAZPACHO

½ pound onions
1 cucumber
2 pounds tomatoes,
   peeled
½ cup red wine
Salt and pepper

3 cloves garlic, crushed
1 tablespoon paprika
3 tablespoons olive oil
12 slices cucumber
12 pitted black olives

Finely chop onions, cucumber, and tomatoes. Pour into blender with wine and salt and pepper to taste. Liquefy ingredients. Pour into bowl and cool.
Blend together in a small bowl the garlic, paprika, and oil until very thick. Slowly stir into cold soup. Add cucumber slices and olives. Allow to chill before serving.

Yield: 4 servings.

PARSON'S SOUP

3 cups chicken broth
½ clove garlic, crushed
1 tablespoon butter
1 tablespoon dried mint
1 tablespoon minced
  parsley

1 teaspoon oregano
1 hard-cooked egg,
  chopped
3 olives, sliced thin

Heat chicken broth. Sauté garlic in butter and add with mint, parsley, and oregano to the soup. Cover and let simmer 10 minutes. Arrange chopped egg and olive slices in 6 bowls and strain the soup into them.

Yield: Approximately 6 small servings.

GRATED POTATO SOUP

3 pints rich ham stock
¼ cup finely chopped
  onion
¾ teaspoon salt
¼ teaspoon ground black
  pepper
2 cloves garlic, crushed

⅛ teaspoon ground
  ginger
1 cup finely shredded
  raw potatoes
1 teaspoon fresh lemon
  juice
Grated Parmesan cheese

Place stock, onion, salt, black pepper, garlic, and ginger in a saucepan. Heat to boiling point. Add potatoes, cover, and boil 5 minutes. Stir in lemon juice. Serve hot with grated Parmesan cheese sprinkled over the top.

Yield: 1¾ quarts.

CALALOO

(A Soup)

⅛ pound salt beef,
 diced
4 large cabbage leaves
6 okra, cut up
⅛ pound salt pork,
 diced
2 cloves garlic, finely cut

2 onions, cut in eighths
⅛ teaspoon thyme
1 quart water
¼ cup canned crabmeat,
 shredded
2 tablespoons butter

Place salt beef on the bottom of a kettle, then line with cabbage leaves. Add okra, salt pork, garlic, onions, thyme, and water and let boil until onions are tender and liquid is reduced to half. Do not stir but shake kettle occasionally. Add crabmeat just before soup is done, allowing time enough for it to heat through. Add butter and beat well with a wire whip.

Yield: Approximately 2 large servings.

ZUPPA DI PESCE ALLA VENEZIANA

(Fish Soup Venetian Style)

2 pounds haddock and
 flounder
3 cups fish stock
½ cup olive oil
2 cloves garlic
1 bay leaf
Pinch thyme
1 tablespoon parsley,
 minced

1 tablespoon fresh basil,
 minced (or ½ teaspoon
 dry basil leaves)
½ cup white wine
2½ cups plum tomatoes
½ teaspoon saffron
Salt and pepper to taste

Have fishman remove heads, tails, and bones from fish, clean skin, and cut fish into 1-inch slices.

Make a fish stock by combining the following ingredients not listed above: 3 cups boiling water, 1 teaspoon salt, 1 small onion, bay leaf, and sprig of parsley. Simmer gently about 30 minutes. Strain stock and reserve.

In a large saucepan, heat olive oil, garlic, bay leaf, and thyme. When garlic is browned, remove and discard. Brown fish in oil mixture. Add fish stock and remaining ingredients. Bring to a boil. Reduce heat to simmer; cook gently 10 to 15 minutes. Serve hot with croutons sautéed in olive oil.

Yield: 6 to 8 servings.

GREEK LENTIL SOUP

2 cups dried lentils	*4 whole cloves*
1 quart water	*2 cloves garlic, quartered*
2 medium-size onions	*1 tablespoon olive oil*
⅛ teaspoon thyme	*2 cups milk*
1½ teaspoons salt	*1 tablespoon wine*
⅛ teaspoon pepper	*vinegar*

Wash and pick over lentils; place in kettle with water and simmer 1 hour. Add 1 finely chopped onion, thyme, salt, and pepper. Push cloves into other onion left whole; place in soup. Continue to simmer 1½ to 2 hours, or until lentils are tender.

In medium-size saucepan, sauté garlic buds in olive oil, removing pieces of garlic when browned.

Remove cloves from onion. Strain soup into saucepan, pressing lentils and onion through sieve. Add milk. Bring soup to boiling point; add vinegar just before serving.

Yield: 6 to 8 servings.

EGG AND MILK SOUP

2 *cloves garlic, minced*	4½ *cups milk*
1 *tablespoon lard*	6 *eggs*
4 *tomatoes*	3 *ounces American*
1 *teaspoon salt*	*cheese*
1 *teaspoon marjoram*	

In large saucepan sauté garlic in lard until golden. Peel tomatoes and slice. Add tomato slices, salt, and marjoram to garlic, bring to a boil, cover, and simmer 10 minutes. Add milk and heat until milk is scalded. Drop eggs into soup carefully by breaking each into a small dish, then slipping quickly into milk. Cover, reduce heat, and let stand for 3 to 5 minutes, or until white of egg is set. Serve in hot soup plates, one egg in each serving, and garnish with diced cheese. *Yield:* Approximately 6 servings.

AIGO-SAOU

(Soup of Provence)

2 *pounds whitefish,*	*Bouquet garni*
cut up	4 *teaspoons salt*
1 *onion, sliced*	*Pepper*
4 *tomatoes, chopped*	2 *quarts water*
4 *potatoes, quartered*	4 *slices of French bread*
2 *cloves garlic*	

Place all ingredients except bread in large kettle. Bring to a boil and cook for 20 to 25 minutes.

Place bread slice in soup bowl. Strain soup and serve over bread slice. Serve fish and potatoes separately, with AIOLI SAUCE.

Yield: 4 servings.

BOURRIDE

(Fish Soup Provençale)

3 pounds cod and
  haddock fillets
1 onion, chopped
⅛ teaspoon thyme
½ teaspoon chopped
  parsley
⅛ teaspoon fennel
½ orange rind, dried

Salt and pepper to taste
1½ quarts hot water
8 cloves garlic, crushed
12 tablespoons olive oil
Juice of 1 lemon
1 tablespoon warm water
Slices of French bread
4 egg yolks

Place fish, onion, thyme, parsley, fennel, orange rind, salt
and pepper, and water in kettle. Boil 10 minutes.

Blend garlic with pinch of salt and pepper. Slowly add
4 tablespoons of oil, beating well. Slowly blend lemon juice
and warm water into garlic. Continue beating and slowly add
remaining 8 tablespoons of oil.

Place a few slices of bread in soup tureen. Strain half of
fish stock into tureen.

Beat egg yolks in a bowl. Slowly add 8 tablespoons of
garlic sauce and blend well. Strain remaining fish stock into
garlic mixture, whisking as you slowly add. Reheat until the
egg yolk-fish stock thickens. When mixture coats the stirring spoon pour the mixture over bread and soup in the
tureen. Serve fish and soup separately.

Yield: 6 to 8 servings.

PISTOU

6 cups water
½ pound string beans,
  cut
3 potatoes, diced
2 tomatoes, peeled and
  diced
Salt and pepper to taste
½ cup noodles or
  spaghetti

3 cloves garlic, crushed
½ teaspoon crushed
  basil leaves
2 tablespoons olive oil
4 tablespoons grated
  Parmesan cheese

Bring water to boil in large kettle. Place string beans, potatoes, tomatoes, salt, and pepper in kettle. Cook over medium heat until potatoes are almost cooked. Add noodles and reduce heat and cook until noodles are ready.

Blend together garlic, basil leaves, and oil in small bowl or mortar. Add 3 tablespoons of soup and blend garlic mixture. Place garlic mixture and cheese in soup tureen. Pour soup into tureen, stirring gently. Serve hot.

Yield: 6 servings.

Meats

O'he's as tedious
As a tired horse, a railing wife;
Worse than a smoky house: I had rather live
With cheese and garlic in a windmill, far,
Than feed on cates and have him talk to me
In any summer house in Christendom.

—*King Henry IV, Shakespeare*

CASSOULET

4 cups pea beans
2 quarts water
3 teaspoons salt
2 cloves garlic, chopped
2 carrots, peeled and
  quartered
2 onions
Bouquet garni of parsley,
  celery leaves, bay leaf,
  thyme, and 2 cloves
  tied in cheesecloth
½ cup diced salt pork
3 tablespoons vegetable
  oil
1 pound lean pork,
  cubed

1 pound lean lamb,
  cubed
1 Bermuda onion,
  chopped
¾ cup shallots, chopped
1 cup sliced celery
1 8-ounce can tomato
  sauce
1 cup dry white wine
1 8-ounce piece hard
  garlic sausage, sliced
1 roasted duck (meat
  removed from bone)

Wash beans and combine with water and salt and let stand overnight in cool place. Add garlic, carrots, onions, bouquet garni, and salt pork. Bring to a boil and let simmer, covered, 1 hour. Skim surface.

Meanwhile, heat oil and brown pork and lamb. Add to bean mixture. Cook Bermuda onion, shallots, and celery until tender, but not browned, in drippings from pork and lamb. Add tomato sauce and wine and bring to a boil. Add with garlic sausage to beans. Cover and simmer until meat and beans are tender, about 1 hour. Add more water, if necessary, to cover beans. Skim off excess fat. Discard bouquet garni. Add salt and fresh-ground pepper to taste. Spoon mixture into a 4-quart casserole. Arrange pieces of duck on bean mixture. Bake in a 350°F. oven 30 to 40 minutes.

Yield: 8 servings.

ROLLED FLANK STEAK WITH
CELERY STUFFING

2 pounds flank steak
1 teaspoon salt
¼ teaspoon ground black
  pepper
2 tablespoons finely
  chopped onion
½ cup finely chopped
  celery
¼ cup butter or
  margarine
2 cups soft bread
  crumbs
1¼ teaspoons salt

½ teaspoon poultry
  seasoning
⅛ teaspoon ground
  black pepper
Flour
1 tablespoon chopped
  beef suet or shortening
¾ cup boiling water
1 tablespoon cornstarch
1 tablespoon water
¹⁄₁₆ teaspoon ginger
1 clove garlic, crushed
¹⁄₁₆ teaspoon black
  pepper

Score flank steak. Mix salt and black pepper and rub into both sides of meat.

Sauté onion and celery in butter or margarine until limp. Add bread crumbs and seasonings. Mix lightly. Spread stuffing evenly over steak and roll lengthwise in jelly-roll fashion. Tie or fasten end with a skewer. Sprinkle lightly with flour. Brown on all sides in beef suet or shortening. Place on a rack in a Dutch oven or baking dish. Add ¾ cup boiling water. Cover and simmer 1½ hours or cook in a 300°F. oven 2 hours.

To serve, place meat on platter. Remove skewers, cut strings, and slice crosswise. Serve with gravy made by mixing cornstarch with the 1 tablespoon water and seasonings. Add to pan juices and cook until thickened.

Yield: 6 servings.

CHILI CON CARNE

2 tablespoons salad oil
2 pounds ground chuck
3 cups water
½ cup finely chopped
  onion
3½ teaspoons salt
3 tablespoons chili
  powder
4 cloves garlic, crushed
1 teaspoon ground cumin
  seed

½ teaspoon oregano
  leaves
¼ teaspoon cayenne
¼ teaspoon ground black
  pepper
1 tablespoon paprika
1 teaspoon sugar
2 tablespoons flour
¼ cup cold water

Heat oil in a 9- or 10-inch skillet. Add meat, stir, and cook until it is gray. Add water, cover, and simmer 30 minutes. DO NOT BOIL. Add onion, seasonings, and sugar. Cook, covered, below boiling point, 15 minutes.

Blend flour with cold water, mixing until smooth. Add and cook until slightly thickened.

If desired, serve with rice and chili beans.

Yield: 6 servings.

BEEF AND SOUR CREAM HUNGARIAN

⅓ cup butter
2 pounds beef round or
  chuck cut into ½-inch
  cubes
1 cup chopped onions

½ teaspoon salt
½ teaspoon pepper
1 clove garlic, crushed
½ cup water
2 cups sour cream

Melt butter in frying pan over low heat. Add beef and onions and brown slowly. Add salt, pepper, garlic, and water.

Cover tightly and simmer over low heat for 1 hour, or until meat is tender.

If needed, additional water may be added during cooking, ½ cup at a time. When tender, stir in sour cream and heat—do not boil—stirring constantly.

Yield: 6 servings.

HUNGARIAN BEEF CASSEROLE

2 tablespoons salad oil
2 onions, finely chopped
2 tablespoons paprika
2 teaspoons salt
2 teaspoons caraway
  seed
1 teaspoon marjoram
  leaves
4 cloves garlic, crushed
¼ teaspoon ground black
  pepper

½ cup ketchup
1½ cups beef broth
3 tablespoons olive oil
3 pounds lean chuck,
  cut into 1½-inch
  pieces
¼ cup flour
1 cup sour cream
Cooked broad noodles

Heat the salad oil in a skillet; add onions and cook over low heat until lightly browned. Blend in paprika, salt, caraway seed, marjoram leaves, garlic, and ground black pepper. Stir in ketchup and beef broth. Heat to boiling; remove from heat and reserve.

In the meantime, heat the olive oil in a deep saucepan. Dredge the meat in the flour and cook, adding a few pieces at a time, until browned on both sides. Add the broth mixture. Bring to a boil, reduce heat, and simmer slowly 2½ hours, or until tender.

Stir in sour cream just before serving. Serve over noodles.

Yield: 6 servings.

DELHI STEAK

1 *pound ground round*
steak
1 *cup water*
1½ *teaspoons ground*
turmeric
½ *cup finely chopped*
onion

1½ *teaspoons salt*
1 *teaspoon ground*
ginger
½ *teaspoon ground red*
pepper
4 *cloves garlic, crushed*

Place all ingredients in a saucepan. Mix well. Stir and cook until very dry, about 30 minutes.

Yield: 4 servings.

SPICED ROAST LEG OF LAMB, GREEK STYLE

6 *to 7 pounds leg of*
lamb
2½ *cloves garlic*
2½ *teaspoons ground*
oregano leaves
1 *clove garlic, crushed*

1 *teaspoon salt*
¼ *teaspoon ground black*
pepper
½ *cup olive oil*
1½ *tablespoons fresh*
lemon juice

Wipe lamb with a damp cloth. Make five slits ½ inch wide and 2 inches deep at intervals over the top of the lamb. Fill each slit with ½ clove garlic.

Mix ½ teaspoon of the oregano, crushed garlic, salt, and ground black pepper and rub over the lamb.

Combine the remaining oregano, olive oil, and lemon juice. Cook 5 minutes. Rub into the lamb.

Place lamb on a rack in a large shallow pan and put into a 325°F. oven. Cook, uncovered, 3 to 3½ hours, basting several times with herbed olive oil and lemon juice. Make a gravy from drippings left in pan. Remove garlic cloves before serving.

Yield: 6 to 8 servings.

SPICY MEAT IN FRIED COCONUT

¾ cup cooked coconut
½ pound round steak,
  cut into 1-inch cubes
1 tablespoon olive oil
¼ cup grated onion
1 clove garlic, grated
2 teaspoons curry
  powder

2 tablespoons brown
  sugar
1 tablespoon lime juice
1 bay leaf, crushed
2 teaspoons salt
¼ cup water
1 tablespoon soy sauce

Brown cooked coconut in fry pan over very low heat until dark golden brown, stirring frequently.

Sauté meat cubes in oil, turning frequently. Add grated onion, clove; continue cooking 5 minutes. Add remaining ingredients; blend well. Cook over low heat about 15 to 20 minutes, or until meat is tender. Add browned coconut, blend well; mixture should be dry.

Yield: 2 servings.

CHOPPED BEEF AND STRING BEANS

1 pound string beans
4 tablespoons salad oil
Dash pepper
1 pound chopped beef
¼ cup finely diced onion

2 cloves garlic, minced
1 cup beef bouillon
3 eggs, slightly beaten
2 tablespoons cornstarch
¼ cup cold water

Cut beans into ¼-inch slices; cook until almost tender. Combine oil and pepper; pour into hot, heavy frying pan. Add beef, onion, and garlic. Cook over moderate heat, stirring constantly, until beef is cooked through. Add string beans and bouillon. Cover and cook over moderate heat about 5 minutes. Add eggs and cook over very low heat until eggs begin to thicken.

Blend cornstarch and water; add. Cook, stirring constantly, until juice thickens. Salt to taste. Serve with hot rice.

Yield: Approximately 4 servings.

DANISH BEEF-LIVER PIES

FILLING:

½ pound beef liver	*½ clove garlic, finely cut*
½ pound ground beef	*1 small onion, chopped*
1 teaspoon salt	*1 egg, slightly beaten*
¼ teaspoon pepper	
3 tablespoons bread crumbs	

Grind liver and ground beef together and add remaining ingredients, mixing thoroughly.

PASTRY:

1¼ cups sifted flour	*½ cup shortening*
¼ teaspoon salt	*3 to 4 tablespoons ice*
¼ teaspoon baking powder	*water*

Mix and sift dry ingredients, cut in shortening until mixture is the consistency of coarse cornmeal. Add sufficient water to moisten. Roll out in 5-inch squares—fill center with meat mixture, fold, and bend into a crescent. Place on ungreased baking sheet in a 375°F. oven 30 to 40 minutes, or until lightly browned.

Yield: 6 crescents.

NICARAGUAN STEW

2 *pounds beef, cut into*	6 *small potatoes*
1-inch cubes	6 *small onions*
1 *clove garlic, minced*	½ *lemon, thinly sliced*
½ *teaspoon ginger*	6 *small zucchini*
3 *tablespoons ketchup*	6 *small ears corn*
1 *teaspoon salt*	2 *tablespoons butter*
Dash pepper	2 *tablespoons flour*
3 *cups water*	

Place beef, garlic, ginger, ketchup, salt and pepper, and 2 cups water in a large kettle, cover, and let simmer 30 minutes, or until meat is almost tender. Add potatoes, onions, and lemon slices and let simmer 20 minutes. Add remaining water, zucchini, and corn and continue cooking 20 minutes longer, or until corn and zucchini are tender. Remove meat and vegetables to platter, centering corn and zucchini in a border of potatoes, onion, and meat. Discard lemon slices. Melt butter, add flour, and stir to a paste. Add liquid from stew, stirring constantly over low heat until smooth and thickened. Continue cooking 5 minutes and pour over potatoes, onion, and beef on platter.

Yield: Approximately 6 servings.

GRILLED SALISBURY STEAK

2 pounds ground chuck
2 teaspoons salt
½ teaspoon thyme leaves
¼ teaspoon ground black
   pepper
1 clove garlic, crushed
½ cup finely chopped
   onion
1 tablespoon parsley
   flakes

1 tablespoon sweet
   pepper flakes
¼ cup water
Flour
Butter or margarine,
   melted
CHILI-TOMATO SAUCE

Combine first 6 ingredients.
Soften parsley and sweet pepper flakes in water and mix with meat. Shape into 6 steaks ¾ inch thick. Sprinkle lightly with flour. Brush both sides with melted butter or margarine. Broil 15 to 18 minutes, turning once to brown both sides. Serve with CHILI-TOMATO SAUCE.

Yield: 6 servings.

CHILI-TOMATO SAUCE:

1½ cups canned tomatoes
3 tablespoons onion
   flakes
1 tablespoon sweet
   pepper flakes

1½ teaspoons salt
½ teaspoon celery salt
¾ teaspoon chili powder
⅛ teaspoon ground
   black pepper

Cook together all ingredients 10 to 12 minutes. Serve over GRILLED SALISBURY STEAK.

Yield: Approximately 1⅓ cups.

HERBED BURGERS

½ pound ground chuck
¼ pound ground veal
¼ pound ground lean
  pork
¼ cup finely chopped
  onion
1 teaspoon salt

¼ teaspoon coarsely
  ground black pepper
1 teaspoon ground
  ginger
1 clove garlic, crushed
3 slices day-old bread
½ cup water
6 hamburger buns

Place first 8 ingredients in a mixing bowl.

Cut bread slices into cubes and soak 3 minutes in water. Squeeze dry. Add to meat, mix thoroughly but lightly.

Shape into 6 patties ½ inch thick. Grill over medium heat 30 minutes, or until well done to cook pork, turning to cook uniformly.

Serve between hamburger buns.

Yield: 6 servings.

BEEF BALLS IN DILLY CREAM

1 pound ground lean
  beef
1 teaspoon salt
¼ teaspoon ground
  black pepper
½ cup fine dry bread
  crumbs
¼ cup finely chopped
  onion
2 tablespoons water
2 tablespoons shortening

1 10½-ounce can cream
  of mushroom soup
1 beef bouillon cube
½ cup boiling water
1 teaspoon dill seed
2 cloves garlic, crushed
1 tablespoon chili sauce
¾ cup sour cream
¼ teaspoon ground black
  pepper
¼ teaspoon salt
Cooked rice

Combine first 6 ingredients. Shape into 1-inch balls. Brown in hot shortening. Add mushroom soup, beef bouillon cube, water, and dill seed. Cover and simmer 10 minutes. Add garlic and chili sauce. Cook 2 minutes. Stir in sour cream, ground black pepper, and salt. Heat *only* until hot. Serve over rice.

Yield: 36 1-inch balls.

ROMAN ROAST LAMB

5- to 6-pound leg of
  lamb roast
Salt and ground black
  pepper
¼ teaspoon crushed red
  pepper
½ teaspoon rosemary
  leaves, crumbled
4 cloves garlic, crushed
2 medium-size tart
  apples
10 slices bacon
3 whole cloves

½ cup olive or salad oil
½ stick (¼ cup) butter
  or margarine
½ cup (4 ounces) diced
  salt pork
½ teaspoon sage leaves
1 cup finely chopped
  onion
1 cup dry white wine or
  1 cup water and slice
  lemon
6 medium-size potatoes,
  peeled

Have butcher bone the leg of lamb. Rub the inside and outside with salt and black pepper. Make 3 small openings in each side of the roast. Fill with a mixture of crushed red pepper, rosemary, and garlic.

Peel and core apples and place inside of lamb cavity along with 4 strips of the bacon and cloves. Close cavity with skewers and lace together with a clean, strong string.

Place oil, butter or margarine, salt pork, and sage in a baking pan large enough to roast lamb. Add onion to the mixture and place lamb over it. Lay the remaining bacon across the top. Place in a 325°F. oven 1 hour.

Pour half the wine or water and lemon slice over lamb. Add potatoes. Continue cooking 2½ hours, or until lamb is tender, basting with pan liquid 4 times. Remove lamb to serving platter. Add remaining wine or stock to the pan liquid. Heat and serve with the lamb. If desired, pour off the fat from pan drippings and thicken drippings with 2 tablespoons flour mixed with ¼ cup water.

Yield: 10 to 12 servings.

TROPICAL MEAL-IN-ONE

1½ pounds lean lamb,
  cut into cubes
2 tablespoons flour
3 tablespoons salad oil
1 clove garlic, minced
2 onions, cut into
  eighths
1 tablespoon
  Worcestershire sauce
1 teaspoon chili powder
1 teaspoon salt
1 quart water

½ cup brown rice,
  sautéed lightly
1 lemon,, sliced very
  thin
1½ cups lima beans
2 cups corn, cut from
  cobs
1 cup hearts of palm
  or celery
3 large tomatoes, cut
  into eighths
3 green peppers, cut
  into pieces

Wipe lamb with damp cloth, roll in flour, and sauté in oil with garlic and onions. When well browned, add Worcestershire sauce, chili powder, salt, and water to cover. Cover pan and let simmer 30 minutes.

Add rice and remaining water and let simmer 10 minutes. Add lemon slices and lima beans and simmer 30 minutes longer. Add remaining ingredients and more water if necessary and let simmer 10 minutes, or until all ingredients are tender and most of liquid is evaporated. Remove lemon slices before serving.

Yield: 6 to 8 servings.

CURRIED LAMB STEW

2 pounds boneless
shoulder of lamb
4 teaspoons curry
powder
1 tablespoon salt
½ teaspoon ground black
pepper
¼ cup flour
2 tablespoons shortening
2 cups water

2 cups cubed potatoes
1 cup sliced carrots
1 cup sliced celery
1 cup finely chopped
onion
2 cloves garlic, crushed
1 cup frozen peas
⅛ teaspoon ground
ginger

Trim excess fat from meat.

Combine curry powder, salt, black pepper, and flour, into which roll meat. Brown on all sides in shortening in a saucepan or Dutch oven. Add water, cover, and cook 1½ hours.

Add potatoes, carrots, celery, onion, and garlic. Cover and cook 20 minutes, or until meat and vegetables are tender. Add peas and ground ginger. Cover and cook 10 minutes, or until peas are done.

Yield: 6 servings.

LAMB CHOPS IN PIQUANT SAUCE

2 tablespoons olive or
  salad oil
2 tablespoons fresh
  lemon juice
1½ teaspoons salt
1 teaspoon ground black
  pepper
1 teaspoon oregano
  leaves
8 cloves garlic, crushed
6 shoulder lamb chops,
  cut ¼ inch thick

4 anchovy fillets,
  chopped
⅛ teaspoon ground
  black pepper
½ teaspoon oregano
  leaves
1 tablespoon cider
  vinegar
½ teaspoon powdered
  mustard
2 teaspoons cold water

Combine oil, lemon juice, salt, black pepper, oregano, and
4 crushed garlic cloves. Rub on all sides of lamb chops. Let
marinate overnight or 3 to 4 hours in refrigerator.

When ready to cook, combine anchovies, remaining garlic,
black pepper, oregano, and vinegar. Combine mustard and
cold water and add. Brush lamb chops on both sides with
the sauce and arrange in a 13×9×2-inch baking pan. Bake
in a 350°F. oven 1 hour and 10 minutes, or until chops are
tender, turning once. *Yield:* 6 servings.

GRILLED LAMB CHOPS

12 loin lamb chops
   (1 inch thick)
¼ cup (½ stick) melted
   butter or margarine
¼ teaspoon ground
   black pepper

4 cloves garlic, crushed
1 teaspoon salt
1 tablespoon parsley
  flakes

Trim and discard excess fat from lamb chops.

Combine butter or margarine, black pepper, garlic, salt, and parsley flakes, into which dip lamb chops. Broil 25 minutes, turning to brown both sides.

Yield: 6 servings, 2 chops each.

LAMB INDIA

¼ cup butter or
   margarine
½ cup finely chopped
   onion
4 cloves garlic, crushed
¼ teaspoon ground
   ginger
6 whole cloves
6 whole cardamom
Stick cinnamon, 2 to 3
   inches long
2 teaspoons ground
   coriander
2 teaspoons ground
   cumin seed

¼ teaspoon ground red
   pepper
1 teaspoon ground
   turmeric
2 teaspoons salt
2 pounds leg or shoulder
   of lamb, cubed
1 cup yoghurt
2 tablespoons tomato
   paste
2 tablespoons chopped
   almonds
Grated coconut

Melt butter or margarine. Stir in onion, garlic, and ginger. Cook until onions are golden brown. Add cloves, cardamom, and cinnamon tied together in a cheesecloth bag, along with remaining spices and salt. Stir and continue cooking 4 to 5 minutes. Add meat, yoghurt, tomato paste, and chopped almonds. Cover and cook 60 minutes, or until meat is tender, cooking uncovered the last 30 minutes to reduce the liquid. Serve hot, sprinkled with coconut.

Yield: 6 servings.

CURRY OF LAMB

*1½ pounds lean lamb,
cut into 1-inch
squares*
*2 tablespoons butter or
margarine*
*¼ cup finely chopped
onion*
*1 tablespoon curry
powder*
2 cloves garlic, crushed

*1 apple, peeled, cored,
and cut into pieces*
*3 tomatoes, peeled and
cut into pieces*
2 cups water or stock
1 teaspoon salt
*⅛ teaspoon ground
black pepper*
3 tablespoons flour

Brown lamb lightly in butter or margarine with onion.
Add curry powder, garlic, apple, tomatoes, water or stock,
salt, and pepper. Stir well.

Simmer, covered, until lamb is tender, about 1½ hours.
Remove lamb. Strain sauce and thicken with flour. Return
meat to sauce. Serve with rice.

Yield: 4 servings.

ONION LAMB LOAF

1 clove garlic, crushed
*¼ cup finely chopped
onion*
*1 tablespoon bacon
drippings*
*1½ pounds ground lean
lamb*
*¼ cup crumbled crisp
bacon*

*1½ cups soft bread
crumbs*
*1 tablespoon parsley
flakes*
*½ teaspoon ground
rosemary*
1½ teaspoons salt
*⅛ teaspoon ground
black pepper*
2 large eggs, beaten

Sauté garlic and onion 2 to 3 minutes, or until limp, in bacon drippings. Mix with remaining ingredients.

Press into a 7½ ×4×2½ -inch loaf pan. Bake in a 350°F. oven 1 hour, or until done. Serve with CURRANT JELLY SAUCE, if desired.

Yield: 6 servings.

CURRANT JELLY SAUCE:

Heat ½ cup currant jelly, ¼ cup water, 2 teaspoons prepared mustard, and 1 tablespoon butter or margarine to the boiling point.

FRICASSEE OF LAMB, POLISH STYLE

3 pounds boneless
  shoulder of lamb
1 teaspoon salt
½ teaspoon ground black
  pepper
2 tablespoons butter or
  margarine
2 cloves garlic, crushed
1 teaspoon grated lemon
  peel
1 teaspoon lemon juice
4 anchovy fillets,
  chopped
8 medium-size fresh
  mushrooms, sliced
2 cups beef stock, or 2
  beef bouillon cubes
  dissolved in 2 cups
  hot water
2 tablespoons flour
3 tablespoons water
4 cups cooked rice

Pour hot water over meat and then drain on paper towels to dry. Cut into 1-inch pieces. Mix salt with black pepper and rub into the meat. Brown in butter or margarine.

Add garlic, lemon peel and juice, anchovies, mushrooms, and stock. Cover and cook 1½ hours, or until meat is tender.

Blend flour with water until smooth and add to meat. Mix well. Stir and cook 1 minute, or until slightly thickened.

Serve with cooked rice. *Yield:* 6 servings.

GRILLED LAMB PATTIES

1½ pounds ground
  shoulder of lamb
1½ teaspoons salt
½ teaspoon rosemary
  leaves
1 clove garlic, crushed

½ teaspoon ground black
  pepper
1½ teaspoons instant
  minced onion
1 large egg, lightly
  beaten

Combine all ingredients. Shape into 6 patties.
Brown on both sides in a greased heavy skillet.

Yield: 6 servings.

LAMB AND VEGETABLE STEW

3 pounds boneless
  shoulder or neck of
  lamb
2 sprigs parsley
1 sprig fresh mint
1 rib celery with leaves
Tops from 1 bunch
  green onions
3 cups water

Salt to taste
1 clove garlic, crushed
¼ cup flour, browned
½ cup cold water
½ teaspoon ground
  thyme
3 large carrots
3 medium-size potatoes
12 small white onions

Trim excess fat from lamb and cut into 2-inch pieces.
Try out a few pieces of the lamb fat. Add meat and brown
on all sides. Pour off fat and save for later use.

Tie parsley, mint, celery, and green onion tops in a bundle
and add to meat. Stir in water and salt. Cover and cook
1 hour, or until meat is half done. Add garlic. Cook, covered,
30 minutes. Remove herb bundle and discard.

Blend flour with the ½ cup water until smooth. Mix with the meat. Add thyme.

Peel carrots and potatoes. Cut carrots into 1-inch pieces and potatoes into slices ⅓ inch thick. Brown on all sides in the fat that was drained from the meat. Place over the top of the meat. DO NOT STIR. Peel onions and add. Cover and cook 15 minutes until vegetables are tender. Serve hot.

Yield: 6 to 8 servings.

ROAST LEG OF LAMB
A LA PUERTO RICO

4- to 5-pound leg of lamb	*1 teaspoon oregano*
1 clove garlic, chopped	*1½ tablespoons olive oil*
¼ teaspoon ground pepper	*4 to 5 teaspoons salt*

Remove skin, excess fat from lamb; wipe meat with damp cloth. Place meat on rack in shallow roasting pan, fat side up. Carefully make superficial crisscross gashes on top of roast.

Place chopped garlic, pepper, oregano in small bowl; crush together with wooden spoon. Add olive oil, salt; blend well. Rub seasoning into meat; cover; place in refrigerator overnight.

Remove from refrigerator ½ hour before cooking. Drain off any liquid that may have seeped from meat; pour over meat. Roast uncovered in a 325°F. oven allowing 35 to 40 minutes per pound, or until meat thermometer registers 182°F. Use pan drippings to make gravy.

Yield: 8 servings.

LAMB AND VEGETABLES

Juice of 2 large lemons	*1 tablespoon salt*
¼ cup olive oil	*2 pounds lamb, cut into*
2 tablespoons grated	*1½-inch cubes*
onion	*8 slices bacon, cut in*
1 tablespoon chili	*half*
powder	*1 large green pepper,*
2 teaspoons curry	*cut into 1-inch pieces*
powder	*4 medium-size onions,*
2 teaspoons ground	*cut in quarters*
ginger	*6 slices pineapple, cut in*
2 teaspoons turmeric	*half*
1 clove garlic, mashed	*4 medium-size tomatoes,*
to a pulp	*cut in quarters*

Combine lemon juice, olive oil, grated onion, chili powder, curry powder, ginger, turmeric, garlic, salt; blend thoroughly. Add lamb cubes; marinate overnight. Wrap half slices bacon around green pepper slices. Place marinated meat onto four 12×14-inch skewers, alternating with pieces of onion, bacon-wrapped green pepper, half pineapple slices, tomato quarters. Place lamb on grill about 3 inches above hot coals or on broiler rack about 3 inches below broiler; barbecue or broil 15 to 20 minutes, turning frequently to brown on all sides. Serve with sauce. *Yield:* 4 servings.

SAUCE:

6 teaspoons prepared	*2 tablespoons soy sauce*
mustard	*2 tablespoons*
2 tablespoons peanut	*Worcestershire sauce*
butter	*Few drops Tabasco*
1 teaspoon turmeric	*sauce*

Combine mustard, peanut butter; make paste. Add turmeric, soy sauce, Worcestershire sauce, Tabasco sauce; blend thoroughly. Serve with lamb. *Yield:* 4 servings.

ROTI D'AGNEAU AUX ANCHOIS

(Roast Leg of Lamb with Herbs and Anchovies)

1 7-pound leg of lamb	*1 large onion, chopped*
4 cloves garlic	*1 leek, chopped*
12 anchovy fillets	*Bouquet garni*
½ teaspoon dry mustard	*2 whole cloves*
Dash pepper, sage,	*1 cup hot water*
marjoram, and thyme	*1½ cups beef stock*
1 large carrot, coarsely	*2 tablespoons tomato*
chopped	*paste*

Lard lamb with garlic and anchovy fillets. Rub surface with dry mustard, pepper, sage, marjoram, and thyme. Place in a shallow roasting pan. Add carrot, onion, leek, bouquet garni, cloves, and water. Roast in a 325°F. oven, 4 hours, basting occasionally.

Strain mixture from roasting pan into a saucepan. Add beef stock and tomato paste; bring to a boil. Serve with lamb.

Yield: 8 to 10 servings.

LAMB SKILLET DINNER

1½ pounds shoulder of	*¾ cup uncooked rice*
lamb	*1½ cups fresh or frozen*
1 clove garlic, split	*peas*
1 tablespoon shortening	*2 tablespoons minced*
2 tablespoons minced	*parsley*
onion	*1½ teaspoons salt*
½ cup diced celery	*¼ teaspoon pepper*
½ pound (2 medium-	*¼ teaspoon basil*
size) tomatoes	*1¾ cups water*

Remove bone and excess fat from meat and cut into small cubes or slices. Brown meat and garlic in heated shortening in large skillet. Remove garlic. Add onion and celery and cook 5 minutes longer, stirring frequently to prevent over-browning.

Remove skin from tomatoes and cut into small pieces. Add to meat. Bring to a boil. Lower heat; cover and simmer slowly for about 30 minutes, or until meat is tender. Add remaining ingredients in order listed. Again bring mixture to a boil and lower heat. Cover and simmer about 20 minutes, or until rice and peas are tender.

Yield: 6 servings.

VEAL PARMIGIANA

1 medium-size onion, finely chopped	*¼ teaspoon basil*
1 clove garlic, crushed	*1 pound veal, cut into 8 pieces, ⅛ inch thick*
7 tablespoons olive oil	
1 1-pound can tomatoes	*1 egg, slightly beaten*
1 8-ounce can tomato sauce	*⅓ cup dry bread crumbs*
1¼ teaspoons salt	*⅔ cup Parmesan cheese*
¼ teaspoon pepper	*½ pound Mozzarella cheese, thinly sliced*
½ teaspoon oregano	

Cook onion and garlic in 2-quart saucepan in 2 tablespoons hot olive oil, until onions are tender. Add tomatoes, tomato sauce, and seasonings. Continue cooking 30 minutes.

Dip veal in egg; coat with combined crumbs and ⅓ cup Parmesan cheese. Cook veal in skillet in remaining 5 tablespoons hot oil until richly brown and tender.

Transfer veal to 12×7½×2-inch baking dish; cover with

two-thirds of tomato mixture; arrange Mozzarella cheese on top; cover with remaining tomato mixture; sprinkle with remaining Parmesan cheese. Bake in a 350°F. oven 30 minutes.

Yield: 4 servings.

FRICASSEE D'AGNEAU

(Lamb and Onion Fricassee)

1 3-pound breast of lamb	*1 cup meat stock*
Seasoned flour	*1 cup red wine*
¼ cup butter	*Bouquet garni*
1 large onion, thinly sliced	*6 peppercorns*
	1 clove garlic
	Cooked noodles

Cut lamb breast into serving portions; roll in seasoned flour.

Melt butter in a deep kettle; brown lamb on both sides. Drain off fat. Add remaining ingredients, except noodles. Bring to a boil; cover. Reduce heat and simmer 2 hours, or until tender, adding additional wine if necessary. Remove bouquet garni and garlic. Serve with cooked noodles.

Yield: 4 servings.

VITELLO TONNATO

(Veal with Tuna Gravy)

⅓ cup olive oil
2 pounds boneless leg of
veal, rolled and tied
¾ cup tuna fish
8 anchovy fillets,
chopped
1 onion, chopped

Salt and pepper to taste
2 cups dry white wine
1 tablespoon chopped
parsley
2 cloves garlic, crushed
½ teaspoon thyme
Hot cooked rice

Heat oil in Dutch oven. Brown veal lightly on all sides.
Add remaining ingredients, except rice, and cover tightly.
Cook over medium heat 1½ to 2 hours, basting occasionally.
Cook until meat is tender. Strain gravy. Serve meat slices
on hot rice. Serve gravy separately.

Yield: 6 servings.

NOTE: May be served cold by pouring strained gravy over meat
and placing in refrigerator overnight.

GUATEMALAN MEAT BALLS

½ pound ground beef
½ pound ground pork
2 tablespoons minced
onion
1 clove garlic, crushed
2 tablespoons bread
crumbs
3 hard-cooked eggs,
chopped

1 tablespoon ketchup
¼ teaspoon allspice
½ teaspoon ginger
½ teaspoon salt
¼ teaspoon chili powder
¼ cup flour
2 tablespoons oil
2 cups beef broth
¼ cup grated cheese

Combine beef, pork, onion, garlic, bread crumbs, eggs, ketchup, and seasonings. Shape into small balls and chill.

Roll in flour and sauté in oil. When browned on all sides, add broth, cover, and let simmer 15 minutes. Turn into casserole with broth, sprinkle with cheese, and place under low broiler heat for 2 to 3 minutes, or until cheese melts and browns slightly.

Yield: Approximately 6 servings.

BREADED PORK CHOPS, SPANISH STYLE

1 cup finely grated bread crumbs	*2 tablespoons oil*
	Salt and pepper
1 clove garlic, crushed	*6 pork chops*
2 tablespoons minced parsley	*1 4-ounce can pimientos*

Make a paste of bread crumbs, garlic, parsley, oil, and salt and pepper. Pound this paste into chops.

Fry chops slowly, until brown and well done.

Serve on hot platter garnished with pimientos which have been sautéed in a little oil or butter.

Yield: 6 servings.

PORK STEAK

½ cup chopped celery
½ cup finely minced
onion
1 medium-size tomato,
chopped
¼ cup chopped
mushrooms
1 clove garlic, finely
minced
¼ cup tomato purée
1 cup white wine

¼ teaspoon chopped
parsley
1 tablespoon flour
1 teaspoon salt
¼ teaspoon sweet basil
¼ teaspoon marjoram
¼ teaspoon thyme
2 pounds pork steaks,
cut into ½×1½-inch
strips
¼ cup cooking brandy
(optional)

Combine celery, onion, tomato, mushrooms, garlic, tomato purée, wine, and parsley in saucepan; blend well.

Combine flour, salt, basil, marjoram, and thyme; stir into tomato mixture; heat to boiling, stirring occasionally. Add pork strips; blend well. Pour into 9-inch casserole. Bake in a 350°F. oven 1 hour and 15 minutes, or until pork is tender. If desired, 5 minutes before removing from oven, stir in brandy. Sauce may be thickened with 2 tablespoons flour.

Yield: 6 servings.

JAMBALAYA

¼ pound salt pork
¼ pound smoked ham
2 onions, minced
1 clove garlic, minced
2½ cups (1-pound
4-ounce can) tomatoes
1 red pepper pod,
chopped

1 pint oysters
1 pound shrimp, shelled
and deveined
3 cups water
2 cups uncooked rice
Salt and pepper to taste

Dice salt pork and ham. Cook slowly in large heavy skillet or Dutch oven until all fat has been fried out. Add onions and garlic and cook until soft. Add tomatoes and pepper and simmer slowly about 1 hour, adding a little water as needed. Add the oysters and their liquor, shrimp, water, and rice. Bring to a boil; lower heat. Cover and cook slowly about 20 minutes, or until rice is tender. Season to taste with salt and pepper.

Yield: 6 to 8 servings.

PORK CHOPS WITH RICE CREOLE

6 *large pork chops*
2 *teaspoons salt*
½ *teaspoon pepper*
1 *tablespoon shortening*
2 *cups sliced onions*
1 *clove garlic, minced*
1 *10½-ounce can
    condensed tomato soup*
2 *cups water*
¼ *cup diced celery*
¼ *cup diced green
    pepper*
2 *tablespoons minced
    parsley*
¾ *cup uncooked rice*
1 *bay leaf, crumbled*
⅛ *teaspoon thyme*
⅛ *teaspoon marjoram*

Season chops with 1 teaspoon of the salt and ¼ teaspoon of the pepper. Brown in shortening. Place chops in bottom of 2½-quart casserole.

Brown onions and garlic in 1 tablespoon of the drippings. Add remaining ingredients and pour over pork chops. Bake in a 350°F. oven 45 to 60 minutes, or until rice is tender.

Yield: 6 servings.

PORK AND CABBAGE CASSEROLE

1½ pounds fresh pork shoulder	1 large bay leaf
1 teaspoon salt	3 sprigs parsley
⅛ teaspoon pepper	1 sprig thyme
1 clove garlic	2 cups diced raw potatoes
3 cups hot water	3 tablespoons chopped parsley
3 cups grated cabbage	

Wipe meat with a damp cloth and cut into 1-inch cubes. Rub with salt and pepper and brown quickly on both sides in a heavy frying pan.

Rub the inside of a deep casserole with garlic. Place pork on the bottom, cover with hot water, add any remaining salt and pepper and cook over low flame for 30 minutes. Add cabbage. Tie bay leaf, parsley, and thyme together with a heavy white thread and add to the pork and cabbage. Top with potatoes, sprinkle with additional salt, cover, and bake in a 350°F. oven 35 minutes, or until potatoes are tender. Remove herbs, sprinkle with chopped parsley, and serve in the casserole.

Yield: 6 servings.

FEIJOADA

3 cups black beans	3 scallions, minced
½ pound dried beef	1 onion, minced
½ pound smoked sausage	2 tablespoons salad oil
½ pound smoked pork	¼ cup fat
¼ pound smoked tongue	½ clove garlic, minced
¼ pound bacon	Dash cayenne

Soak beans in water to cover overnight. Drain. Cover beans and beef with fresh cold water and simmer 2 hours. Place sausage, pork, tongue, and bacon in the same kettle. Simmer until the beans are soft enough to mash easily.

Sauté scallions and onion in salad oil and fat until soft and yellow. Add garlic and cayenne, continue cooking until delicately browned.

Remove half the beans from kettle and add to onion mixture, stir until these beans are well mashed. Return the mashed beans to the kettle and simmer until the mixture thickens, but be sure the mixture is not thicker than an ordinary cream soup. Remove meats, slice and arrange on a platter. Pour a little of the bean mixture over the slices and serve the rest in a deep vegetable dish or tureen. Rice is always served as an accompaniment.

Yield: Approximately 6 servings.

COSTOLETTE DI MAIALE PIZZAIOLA

(Pork Chops Pizzaiola)

2 *cloves garlic*	3 *tablespoons olive oil*
6 *pork chops, ½ to ¾ inch thick*	½ *cup tomato sauce*
	¼ *cup dry red wine*
Salt and pepper	¼ *teaspoon oregano*
2 *green peppers, cut in squares*	3 *sausages, sliced*
½ *pound mushrooms, sliced*	

Rub garlic over chops and spice with salt and pepper. Brown green peppers and mushrooms in oil, then add chops and brown on both sides. Add tomato sauce, wine, and oregano, then cover and cook over low heat until pork is tender.

Brown sausages in separate skillet. Drain and place in with chops. Stir gently over low heat 2 to 3 minutes, then serve.

Yield: 6 servings.

Barbecue Meats and Poultry

Wel loved he garleek, oynons, and eek lekes,
And for to drinken strong wyn, reed as blood.

—*Chaucer*

SPICY BEEF KEBABS

1½ pounds sirloin tip
18 small white onions
SPICY BARBECUE SAUCE

Cut beef into 1½-inch cubes.
Peel onions and parboil 10 minutes in boiling salted water, using 1 teaspoon salt to 1 quart boiling water.
String beef and onions alternately on skewers. Brush with SPICY BARBECUE SAUCE. Cook over a very low charcoal fire until the meat is of desired doneness, turning and basting with barbecue sauce as often as the meat looks dry. (Cooking time depends upon the degree of doneness desired and the heat of the fire. Slow cooking and frequent basting produce a kebab of better flavor.)

Yield: 6 servings.

SPICY BARBECUE SAUCE:

¾ cup fresh lemon juice
½ cup cider vinegar
⅓ cup tomato ketchup
¼ cup salad oil
⅓ cup water
1½ tablespoons light
  brown sugar
2 teaspoons salt

1½ teaspoons powdered
  mustard
¾ teaspoon cayenne
2 tablespoons finely
  chopped onion
¼ teaspoon mashed
  clove garlic

Combine all ingredients in a saucepan. Bring to boiling point and boil 1 minute. Sauce will keep several weeks if stored in a covered jar in the refrigerator.

CUMIN BEEF KEBABS

⅓ cup salad oil
1 tablespoon fresh lemon
juice
2 tablespoons cider
vinegar
2 teaspoons salt
¼ teaspoon ground cumin
seed
¼ teaspoon ground black
pepper

½ cup finely chopped
onion
2 cloves garlic, crushed
1 teaspoon ground
coriander
¼ teaspoon ground
ginger
1½ pounds boneless
round or sirloin steak,
cut ¾ inch thick

Combine oil, lemon juice, vinegar, salt, and spices.

Trim excess fat from beef and cut meat into 1½-inch squares. Add to the spiced mixture. Coat all sides of meat well. Marinate at room temperature 2 to 3 hours.

String meat on skewers. Cook over slow-burning charcoal fire until meat is done, basting with marinade as often as meat looks dry. Cooking time depends upon heat of fire.

Yield: 4 servings.

BAY LEAF KEBABS

2½ pounds London broil
or sirloin tip
2 tablespoons water
⅓ cup salad oil
½ cup cider vinegar
½ cup finely chopped
onion

2 cloves garlic, crushed
1½ teaspoons salt
½ teaspoon ground black
pepper
Bay leaves

Cut meat into 1½-inch cubes, trimming off excess fat. Combine next 7 ingredients. Crumble 2 bay leaves and add. Heat and pour over meat. Marinate 4 to 5 hours or overnight. String meat on skewers, alternating with whole bay leaves. Cook on the grill over low heat until of desired doneness.

Yield: 6 servings.

SPICED BEEF KEBABS

2 tablespoons finely chopped beef suet
2 tablespoons ground coriander seed
½ cup finely chopped onion
1 tablespoon brown sugar
1 teaspoon salt
¼ teaspoon ground black pepper
⅛ teaspoon ground cayenne
2 cloves garlic, crushed
½ teaspoon ground cumin seed
3 tablespoons fresh lemon juice
4 tablespoons soy sauce
2½ pounds round or sirloin steak

Blend together all ingredients except steak. Mix well.

Cut steak into 1½-inch squares. Add to the sauce and let marinate overnight or 3 to 4 hours.

String meat on skewers and broil over a charcoal fire, turning to cook uniformly on all sides. Baste often while cooking with the marinade that is left in the bowl. If desired, string vegetables such as green pepper squares, tomatoes, or other vegetables suitable for kebab grilling on skewers and grill while kebabs are cooking.

Serve in frankfurter buns or, if desired, in long hero buns.

Yield: Approximately 10 servings.

BARBECUED BEEF KEBABS

2 *pounds boneless rump*
  or top round beef
1 *teaspoon powdered*
  mustard
2 *tablespoons water*
¼ *cup finely chopped*
  onion
2 *tablespoons ketchup*
2 *teaspoons salt*

1 *teaspoon sugar*
1 *teaspoon ground black*
  pepper
2 *cloves garlic, crushed*
¼ *teaspoon ground red*
  pepper
¼ *cup salad oil*
½ *cup cider vinegar*

Trim off and discard excess fat from meat, if there is any. Cut meat into 1½-inch squares.

Mix mustard with water and let stand 10 minutes for flavor to develop. Add the remaining ingredients and pour over meat. Marinate overnight or 4 to 5 hours.

String meat on skewers. Cook over a very slow-burning charcoal fire 50 to 60 minutes, or until meat is tender and browned, basting with the sauce as often as meat looks dry.

Yield: 6 to 8 servings.

CURRIED BEEF KEBABS

2 *pounds sirloin steak,*
  sirloin tip, or top
  round
½ *cup finely chopped*
  onion
2 *cloves garlic, crushed*

2 *teaspoons salt*
1 *teaspoon ground black*
  pepper
2 *teaspoons curry powder*
1 *tablespoon lemon juice*
3 *tablespoons salad oil*

Trim and discard excess fat from beef and cut meat into 1-inch cubes. Combine remaining ingredients. Add beef, mix well, and marinate 3 to 4 hours.

String on skewers and cook over a slow-burning charcoal fire until meat is tender and browned, approximately 40 minutes, basting with the marinade as often as kebabs look dry.

Yield: 6 servings.

ONION BEEF KEBABS

2 *pounds sirloin beef*
2 *teaspoons salt*
1 *teaspoon chili powder*
½ *teaspoon poultry*
    seasoning
½ *teaspoon oregano leaves*
½ *teaspoon ground*
    ginger
¼ *teaspoon ground black*
    pepper
1 *small clove garlic, cut*
    in half
2 *tablespoons finely*
    chopped fresh onion

2 *tablespoons fresh lemon*
    juice
1 *tablespoon cider*
    vinegar
½ *cup salad oil*
12 *small white onions,*
    grilled
12 *medium-size*
    mushroom caps, grilled
12 *cherry tomatoes,*
    grilled

Cut beef into 1½-inch cubes and place in a bowl.

Combine salt, spices, garlic, onion, lemon juice, vinegar, and oil. Pour over beef. Marinate in refrigerator overnight or 3 to 4 hours at room temperature.

String meat on skewers. Broil over charcoal grill 15 to 20 minutes, turning skewers frequently to brown on all sides. Baste with marinade while cooking as often as meat looks dry.

Peel onions and parboil 5 minutes in boiling water to cover with 1 teaspoon salt added. String on skewers.

Wash mushrooms and remove stems. String mushroom

caps on a separate skewer. Save stems to use in sauces and soups.

String cherry tomatoes on a skewer. Baste vegetables with the marinade and place over charcoal grill, about 10 minutes before meat has finished cooking. Baste and cook until meat and vegetables are done.

Serve grilled vegetables, allowing 2 pieces beef, 1 onion, 1 mushroom cap, and 1 cherry tomato per serving.

Yield: 12 servings.

EXTRA SPECIAL HAMBURGERS

1 tablespoon sweet pepper flakes	*½ teaspoon powdered mustard*
1 tablespoon water	*½ teaspoon salt*
1 pound ground lean beef	*1½ tablespoons wine vinegar*
⅓ cup ketchup	*1½ tablespoons salad or olive oil*
1 teaspoon onion salt	
¼ teaspoon garlic salt	*4 hamburger buns*

Reconstitute sweet pepper flakes in water for 10 minutes and combine with beef, spices, vinegar, and oil.

Shape into 4 patties. Broil over charcoal fire 45 minutes, or until done, turning to brown both sides.

If desired, broil under oven broiler.

Serve between warmed, split hamburger buns.

Yield: 4 servings.

SPICED CHEESE HAMBURGERS

*1½ pounds lean ground
beef (chuck)
¾ cup finely chopped
onion
2 cloves garlic, crushed
1 teaspoon powdered
mustard*

*1½ teaspoons salt
¼ teaspoon ground black
pepper
Crumbled Roquefort
cheese
6 hamburger buns*

Combine first 6 ingredients. Shape into 12 thin patties, 4 inches in diameter. Place 1½ teaspoons crumbled Roquefort cheese in center of 6 of the patties. Cover with remaining patties, pressing edges together well to keep cheese in place. Brown on both sides in a hot, greased heavy skillet or over a slow-burning charcoal fire.

Serve between warm, split buttered hamburger buns.

Yield: 6 servings.

POLYNESIAN HAMBURGERS

*1½ pounds ground lean
chuck
½ teaspoon instant
onion powder
½ cup soy sauce*

*½ teaspoon ground
ginger
¼ teaspoon ground
black pepper
1 clove garlic, crushed
6 hamburger buns*

Mix beef with instant onion powder. Shape into 6 patties of equal size. Place in a deep dish or baking pan.

Combine next 4 ingredients and pour over meat. Marinate 30 minutes.

Remove from sauce and broil 7 minutes on one side and 4 minutes on other side.

Serve between warm hamburger buns. *Yield:* 6 servings.

HAMBURGER KEBABS

*1½ pounds ground
  chuck*
¼ teaspoon garlic salt
½ teaspoon onion salt
½ teaspoon celery salt
*¼ teaspoon ground
  black pepper*
*12 1-inch pieces green
  pepper*

*12 1-inch pieces fresh
  tomato*
*12 1-inch pieces
  Bermuda onion*
*12 canned mushroom
  buttons, if desired*
3 tablespoons salad oil

Combine meat with seasoning salts and ground black pepper. Form into 1½-inch balls.

Thread on skewer, alternating with the vegetables. Brush with salad oil and broil over hot charcoal. These kebabs may also be cooked in the oven broiler.

Yield: 6 servings.

SPICY BARBECUED MEAT

4 small onions
2 cloves garlic
½ teaspoon red pepper
*1 tablespoon dark brown
  sugar*
1 teaspoon lime juice
*1½ teaspoons curry
  powder*
*½ teaspoon ground
  clove*

*½ teaspoon ground
  ginger*
*3 tablespoons warm
  water*
*3 tablespoons soy
  sauce*
*1½ pounds round
  steak, cut into ¾-inch
  cubes*
PEANUT SAUCE

Grind together onions and garlic; add red pepper, brown sugar, lime juice, curry powder, clove, and ginger; blend well.

Combine water and soy sauce; add to spices; mix thoroughly. Add meat cubes; knead meat with hands to absorb sauce; refrigerate 6 hours. Thread 5 to 6 pieces of marinated meat on each of 10 skewers; place on broiler rack 3 inches away from heat; broil 15 to 20 minutes, brushing meat with sauce and turning frequently. Serve with PEANUT SAUCE.

Yield: 5 to 6 servings.

PEANUT SAUCE:

2 tablespoons grated onion	1 teaspoon lime juice
2 tablespoons olive oil	¼ cup peanut butter
1 tablespoon dark brown sugar	1 cup COCONUT WATER
	Dash salt

Sauté onion in olive oil 5 to 10 minutes; add brown sugar, lime juice, peanut butter; blend well. Gradually add COCONUT WATER, stirring constantly; add salt. Cook until sauce is thick and smooth.

Yield: 1¼ cups.

COCONUT WATER:

1 cup boiling water
1 cup unsweetened coconut

Pour boiling water over coconut. Allow to stand 20 minutes. Strain.

Yield: 1 cup coconut water.

WINE 'N' HONEY SPARERIBS

1 large rack (2½   *½ cup red wine vinegar*
  pounds) spareribs   *1 teaspoon*
1 8-ounce can tomato   *hickory-smoked salt*
  sauce   *½ teaspoon garlic salt*
¼ cup red dinner wine   *⅛ teaspoon ground*
2 tablespoons honey   *clove*
2 tablespoons salad oil

Wipe spareribs well; place in a shallow glass pan.

Combine tomato sauce, wine, honey, and salad oil until blended.

In a small jar with a tightly fitting lid, shake red wine vinegar, hickory-smoked salt, garlic salt, and clove. Stir into tomato mixture. Pour over spareribs; cover and refrigerate overnight. Remove from refrigerator ½ hour before ready to barbecue. Cook over glowing coals 1½ to 2 hours, basting frequently. *Yield:* 4 servings.

BARBECUED LEG OF LAMB

2 cups dry red wine   *1 teaspoon fresh ground*
⅔ cup salad oil   *pepper*
2 cloves garlic,   *½ teaspoon nutmeg*
  minced   *8 whole cloves*
2 small onions, minced   *Parsley*
1 teaspoon powdered   *1 6-pound leg of lamb,*
  mustard   *boned and rolled*
1 teaspoon salt

Combine all ingredients. Marinate lamb overnight or for several hours, turning frequently.

Place on spit according to manufacturer's directions and place over hot coals when heat registers 350°F. Attach the motor and cook lamb 1¾ to 2 hours at 350°F. Baste with marinade frequently when cooking.

Remove from spit when done and slice for serving.

Yield: 8 to 10 servings.

LAMB ON A SKEWER

1 pound ground lean
  lamb
1 teaspoon salt
½ clove garlic, crushed
½ teaspoon ground
  black pepper

2 tablespoons finely
  chopped onion
2 tablespoons dry
  bread crumbs
1 large egg, lightly
  beaten
2 tablespoons salad oil

Combine all ingredients. Shape meat into 1-inch balls. Brush well with additional oil and thread on skewers. Cook over a slow-burning charcoal fire.

Yield: 6 servings, 5 balls per serving.

ROUND STEAK ALFREDO

1 2½-pound piece
  bottom round steak
½ cup red wine vinegar
⅓ cup salad oil

¼ cup ruby port
1 teaspoon hot mustard
1 teaspoon garlic salt
Pepper

Score the fat edge of steak to prevent curling during barbecuing. Turn into a shallow glass pan.

Combine vinegar, oil, port, hot mustard, garlic salt, and

¼ teaspoon pepper. Pour over steak. Cover and refrigerate overnight.

Remove from refrigerator ½ hour before barbecuing. Place over hot, glowing coals, brush with marinade, and sprinkle heavily with pepper. Baste occasionally; cook 20 minutes. Turn steak, baste, and sprinkle with pepper, continue cooking 15 more minutes (for rare).

Yield: 4 servings.

SHEEKH KEBAB

2 pounds sirloin or lean lamb	2 teaspoons ground turmeric
Boiling water	2 teaspoons poppy seeds
6 tablespoons yoghurt	¼ teaspoon cayenne
1 teaspoon ground ginger	2 cloves garlic, crushed
1 cup finely chopped onion	2 teaspoons salt
4 teaspoons ground coriander	¼ cup vegetable oil or melted shortening

Trim excess fat from meat and cut into 1-inch pieces. Cover with boiling water and soak for 5 minutes. Drain.

Combine yoghurt and seasonings to form a paste. Mix with meat and marinate at least 1 hour. String on skewers. Place under broiler or on a grill 5 to 7 minutes, or until meat is cooked, basting well with vegetable oil or melted shortening.

Yield: 6 servings.

LAMB SHISH KEBABS

1 teaspoon onion salt
1 teaspoon celery salt
1 teaspoon garlic salt
¼ teaspoon ground
* black pepper*
½ teaspoon poultry
* seasoning*
1 teaspoon powdered
* mustard*

¼ cup salad oil
2 tablespoons cider
* vinegar*
1½ pounds lean
* boneless leg of lamb*
1 zucchini squash, cut
* into ¾-inch slices*
8 fresh mushroom caps
8 tomato wedges

Combine first 8 ingredients. Cook only until hot. Cool. Trim excess fat from lamb, cut into 1½-inch cubes, and add to marinade. Refrigerate 6 to 8 hours or overnight.

When ready to cook, string lamb on skewers, alternating with squash and mushrooms. Grill over hot embers 15 to 20 minutes, or until done, basting with marinade sauce as often as the meat appears dry. Add tomato wedges when meat is half done.

Yield: 8 servings.

BARBECUED CHICKEN MONTEREY

1 broiler-fryer chicken,
  cut up
¾ cup oil
1 clove garlic, crushed
3 tablespoons prepared
  hot mustard
2 teaspoons salt
¼ teaspoon freshly
  ground pepper

1 teaspoon chili
  powder
½ teaspoon sugar
2 tablespoons lemon
  juice
8 cling peach halves,
  drained

Wash and dry chicken pieces.

In a large bowl, mix oil with seasonings and lemon juice. Put chicken pieces in bowl and turn to coat all sides with marinade. Cover and marinate in refrigerator at least 2 hours, longer if possible.

When ready to barbecue, remove pieces of chicken from marinade. Place on grill over charcoal coals and cook 20 to 30 minutes, turning to cook both sides. Baste two or three times with remaining marinade during cooking.

Five minutes before chicken is done, place peach halves on grill, brush with marinade. Serve hot with chicken.

Yield: 4 servings.

FRENCH GOLDEN CHICKEN

1 broiler-fryer chicken,
  whole
2 teaspoons monosodium
  glutamate
½ teaspoon crushed
  rosemary

2 cloves garlic, crushed
½ teaspoon grated
  lemon peel
½ teaspoon paprika
¼ cup sweet vermouth
¼ cup light salad oil

Wipe and dry chicken well; sprinkle inside cavity with 1 teaspoon monosodium glutamate. Truss and tie chicken; secure tightly on spit.

Combine remaining teaspoon monosodium glutamate, rosemary, garlic, lemon peel, paprika, vermouth, and oil in a small jar. Shake well to blend. When coals are hot and glowing, engage spit in motor and begin cooking. Baste frequently with vermouth mixture. Lower hood partway over rotisserie and cook 45 minutes to 1 hour. (If rotisserie has no hood, make one by shaping two large pieces of aluminum foil into a beehive over spit and coals. Be sure to leave an open area at each end for a free air flow and easy access for basting.) *Yield:* 4 servings.

CHICKEN PUEBLO

2 *broiler-fryer*	¼ *cup garlic-flavored*
chickens, halved	*red wine vinegar*
1 *8-ounce can tomato*	1 *teaspoon*
sauce	*hickory-smoked salt*
¼ *cup salad oil*	1 *teaspoon onion powder*
1 *tablespoon finely*	½ *cup grated sharp*
chopped green chilies	*Cheddar cheese*
	Finely shredded lettuce

Wipe chicken well.

Combine tomato sauce, oil, chilies, garlic vinegar, hickory-smoked salt, and onion powder in a deep china bowl; blend well. Add chicken halves, mixing until each is well coated with tomato mixture. Cover and refrigerate to marinate overnight. Allow to come to room temperature before ready to grill.

When coals are hot and glowing, place chicken on grill and baste well with marinade. Grill 35 to 45 minutes, until browned and done. About 5 minutes before removing from grill, sprinkle each chicken half (skin-side up) with 2 tablespoons grated Cheddar cheese. Allow cheese to just melt. Serve at once on bed of crisp shredded lettuce.

Yield: 4 servings.

MEDITERRANEAN GRILLED CHICKEN

2 *large broiler-fryer*
   chickens, halved
½ *cup olive oil*
½ *cup white dinner*
   wine
¼ *cup honey*
¼ *cup white wine*
   vinegar

2 *teaspoons garlic salt*
1 *teaspoon monosodium*
   glutamate
½ *teaspoon oregano*
1 *large lemon, thinly*
   sliced
1 *large orange, thinly*
   sliced

Wipe chicken well. Combine all remaining ingredients in a deep glass bowl until blended. Add chicken, making sure each piece is covered with marinade. Cover bowl and refrigerate to marinate overnight. Allow to come to room temperature before grilling.

When coals are hot and glowing, place chicken on grill, basting well with marinade. Grill 35 to 45 minutes, until golden brown and done. Serve at once.

Yield: 4 servings.

SESAME CHICKEN TERIYAKI

4 *large boned chicken*
   breasts
¼ *cup soy sauce*
¼ *cup light salad oil*
½ *cup dry sherry*
1½ *teaspoons garlic salt*

¼ *teaspoon ground*
   ginger
1 *10-ounce jar kumquats*
3 *small limes, thinly*
   sliced
Sesame seeds

Remove all chicken skin. Cut chicken breasts into thin strips.

Combine soy sauce, oil, sherry, garlic salt, and ginger in a pint jar, shake well to blend. Turn into a small glass bowl; stir in chicken strips. Cover and marinate overnight.

Start fire in barbecue about ½ hour before ready to grill chicken. Meanwhile, prepare skewers by threading one end of a chicken strip on a short skewer, then a kumquat, then the other end of chicken strip. Thread skewer with a lime and repeat chicken and kumquat. Begin on the next skewer and thread in the same manner until all chicken has been used. Brush skewers with marinade and sprinkle with sesame seeds. When coals are glowing, place skewers on grill. Baste often as the skewers are turned. Chicken will be cooked, but moist, in 12 to 18 minutes. Serve at once.

Yield: 4 servings.

CHICKEN MAHARANI

6 large boned chicken breasts	*1 teaspoon chopped parsley*
½ cup cracked wheat	*½ teaspoon salt*
2 tablespoons melted butter	*¼ cup toasted pine nuts*
1 cup water	*¼ cup golden raisins*
1 chicken bouillon cube	LEMON MARINADE

LEMON MARINADE:

⅔ cup olive oil	*1 teaspoon chopped fresh mint*
½ cup fresh lemon juice	
2 teaspoons garlic salt	*1 teaspoon black pepper*
	1 lemon, thinly sliced

Flatten chicken breasts slightly by pounding with a meat mallet or the edge of a saucer.

Add wheat to butter in a small saucepan, stirring until each kernel is completely coated. Stir in water, chicken bouillon, parsley, and salt. Bring mixture to a boil. Cover and simmer on lowest heat ½ hour, or until all moisture is absorbed. Remove from heat, stir in pine nuts and raisins; cool.

Meanwhile, prepare lemon marinade by combining ingredients and turning into a deep china bowl. When wheat mixture is cool, spoon about 2 tablespoons onto each flattened chicken breast. Roll each, pulling skin over all until the filling is completely enclosed. Skewer tightly with sharp metal turkey skewers. Place stuffed chicken breasts in lemon marinade, turning until each is well coated. Cover and refrigerate overnight. Remove ½ hour before ready to barbecue.

When coals are hot and glowing, place stuffed chicken breasts on grill. Baste with marinade and turn frequently. Cook 45 minutes to 1 hour, until golden brown and done.

Yield: 6 servings.

MARINATED PORK KEBABS

2½ tablespoons ground
    coriander seed
¼ teaspoon cayenne
¼ teaspoon ground
    ginger
¼ teaspoon ground
    black pepper
2 cloves garlic, minced
½ cup finely chopped
    onion

1½ teaspoons salt
1½ tablespoons brown
    sugar
3½ tablespoons fresh
    lemon juice
4½ tablespoons soy sauce
2 pounds boneless lean
    pork

Combine spices, garlic and onion, salt, brown sugar, lemon juice, and soy sauce.

Trim excess fat from pork and cut into 1½-inch cubes. Add to marinade. Let stand 3 to 4 hours.

String on skewers and broil over a slow-burning charcoal fire until well done and browned. (Cooking time depends upon heat of fire.) Baste often with salad oil or melted butter or margarine while cooking.

Yield: 6 servings.

BARBECUED SPARERIBS

3 pounds spareribs
Salt
Fresh lemon slices
Thin onion slices
⅓ cup fresh lemon juice
¼ cup cider vinegar
3 tablespoons ketchup
3 tablespoons water
1 tablespoon brown sugar

1 teaspoon salt
1½ teaspoons powdered mustard
1 teaspoon ground red pepper
½ teaspoon ground black pepper
1 teaspoon finely chopped onion
1 clove garlic, split

Cut spareribs into serving-size pieces and sprinkle with salt. Place in a shallow baking pan, meaty side up. On each place a slice of lemon and then a slice of onion. Roast in a 450°F. oven 30 minutes. Drain off fat.

Combine remaining ingredients. Bring to boiling point. Pour over ribs. Reduce heat to 350°F. and continue cooking 45 minutes, or until tender. Baste ribs with sauce every 15 minutes.

Yield: 3 to 4 servings.

BARBECUED SPARERIBS,
ORIENTAL STYLE

*2 tablespoons brown
 sugar
3 tablespoons ground
 coriander seed
1 tablespoon salt
1 tablespoon chili
 powder
¼ cup finely chopped
 onion
4 cloves garlic, minced
1 teaspoon coarsely
 ground black pepper*

*1 teaspoon ground ginger
2 tablespoons lemon
 juice
2 tablespoons wine
 vinegar
¼ cup soy sauce
¼ cup cooking sherry
4 pounds lean pork
 spareribs*

Combine all ingredients except spareribs. Rub on all sides of the meat.

Arrange ribs in a large platter or shallow baking pan over which pour all excess marinade. Let stand 3 to 4 hours or overnight.

To cook, arrange spareribs in a jelly-roll pan or other large pan. Bake in a 350°F. oven 1½ hours, or until ribs are tender and brown, basting with the marinade five times as the meat cooks. Serve hot.

Yield: 4 servings.

Poultry

He who wears a clove of garlic need not fear the evil eye.

—*Ancient Chinese saying*

ARROZ CON POLLO

1 teaspoon oregano
¼ teaspoon black
　pepper or 2
　peppercorns
1 clove garlic, chopped
1 tablespoon salt
2 teaspoons olive oil
1 teaspoon vinegar
1 broiler-fryer chicken,
　cut into pieces
3 tablespoons shortening
½ cup cooked ham
¼ cup salt pork or 1
　strip uncooked bacon

1 onion
1 green pepper, seeded
6 green olives, pitted
1 teaspoon capers
1 tomato
3 tablespoons tomato
　sauce
2¼ cups uncooked rice
1 17-ounce can green
　peas
1 quart boiling water
1 4-ounce can pimientos

In small bowl, using wooden spoon, mash together oregano, pepper or peppercorns, garlic, salt, olive oil, and vinegar. Rub on chicken.

Melt shortening in Dutch oven; brown chicken lightly over medium-high heat.

Chop ham, salt pork or bacon, onion, green pepper, olives, capers, tomato; add to chicken; reduce heat to medium; cover; cook 10 minutes. Add tomato sauce, rice; cook 5 minutes.

Drain liquid from peas; reserve peas for later use. Add liquid from peas, boiling water; mix well; cook uncovered over medium heat 15 minutes. Mix well; cover and simmer 20 minutes. Add peas; mix well; cover, simmer 10 minutes.

Cut pimientos into strips; heat; drain; use as a garnish.

Yield: 4 servings.

CHICKEN BAKED IN FRESH CORN

1 broiler-fryer chicken	1 cup sliced onions
¼ cup olive oil	2 cups corn cut from
1 clove garlic, ground	cob
2 teaspoons salt	2 eggs, beaten
1 cup minced green	2 cups water
peppers	

Cut chicken into pieces for serving and brown on all sides in oil. Add the seasonings, peppers, and onions and place in casserole.

Mix corn with eggs and water and pour over chicken. Bake in a 375°F. oven about 20 minutes until sauce is firm.

Yield: 2 to 3 servings.

CHICKEN CASSOULET

1 broiler-fryer chicken	¼ pound fresh
¼ cup seasoned flour	mushrooms, washed
6 tablespoons salad oil	½ cup dry sherry or
1 small onion, sliced	white wine
1 clove garlic, crushed	1 cup chicken broth or
4 stalks celery, cut into	consommé
1-inch slices	1 teaspoon salt
4 medium-size carrots,	Ground black pepper
cut into 1-inch slices	
1 green pepper, cut into	
1-inch cubes	

Cut up chicken into serving pieces. Wash well. Place in paper bag with flour; close bag and shake vigorously. Brown floured chicken well in salad oil. Remove chicken to casserole.

Sauté lightly the onion, garlic, celery, carrots, green pepper, and mushrooms in fat left in skillet; add to casserole with chicken. Add dry sherry or white wine and hot chicken broth or consommé. Sprinkle with salt and pepper. Cover tightly and bake at 325°F. 1 hour, or until tender.

Yield: 4 servings.

ASOPAO

1 tablespoon olive oil	*1 small bottle stuffed*
2 slices bacon, quartered	*olives*
1 cup diced smoked ham	*1 clove garlic*
1 pimiento, chopped	*1 6- to 8-pound fowl*
1 large tomato,	*cut for fricassee*
quartered	*1 tablespoon salt*
1 large onion,	*¼ teaspoon pepper*
quartered	*1½ cups rice*
1 red pepper, thinly sliced	*1 cup canned tiny*
in strips	*green peas*

Heat oil in deep saucepan. Add bacon, ham, pimiento, tomato, onion, red pepper, olives, and garlic. Sauté for five minutes.

Add chicken, season with salt and pepper and let brown slightly. Cover with water, cover, and let simmer 2 hours, or until chicken is about tender. Add rice that has been thoroughly washed. Cook rapidly, uncovered, for 7 minutes. Cover, lower heat, and let simmer 15 minutes longer. Stir occasionally with a fork to prevent sticking, being careful not to break chicken. Add peas and simmer 5 minutes longer.

Turn out onto a platter or pottery dish. Garnish with

pimiento cut to look like poinsettia leaves, with sieved egg as the center of the flower.

Yield: 6 servings.

CHICKEN WITH ALMONDS

1 broiler-fryer chicken,
cut into serving pieces
3 tablespoons butter or
margarine
1 clove garlic, minced
2 tablespoons finely
chopped onion
2 tablespoons flour
1 tablespoon tomato
paste or ketchup

1½ cups chicken broth
2 tablespoons cooking
sherry (optional)
2 tablespoons slivered
almonds
¼ teaspoon salt
⅛ teaspoon pepper
¾ cup sour cream
1 tablespoon grated
Parmesan cheese

Brown chicken in hot butter or margarine in skillet. Remove chicken; add garlic and onion; cook 2 to 3 minutes. Stir in flour and tomato paste or ketchup; stir in chicken broth gradually; cook, stirring constantly, until mixture thickens and boils. Blend in sherry if desired and cook 1 minute; stir in almonds, salt, and pepper. Add chicken; cover, continue cooking 45 minutes.

Transfer chicken to shallow heatproof 12×8×2-inch baking dish.

Stir sour cream into gravy; pour over chicken; sprinkle with cheese. Place broiler pan without grid in broiling compartment 5 inches from tip of flame. Preheat 5 minutes at broiling temperature. Place baking dish in broiler pan; broil 2 minutes, or until golden brown.

Yield: 4 servings.

INDIAN CURRIED CHICKEN

1 3- to 4-pound ready-to-cook roasting chicken
½ cup minced onion
1 clove garlic, minced
2½ tablespoons ground coriander seed
1 tablespoon ground turmeric
2½ teaspoons ground cumin seed
1 teaspoon ground ginger

¾ teaspoon ground black pepper
¾ teaspoon ground red pepper
1 tablespoon salad oil
2 tablespoons cider vinegar
2 bay leaves
1 stick cinnamon, 2 inches long
2½ teaspoons salt
¼ cup salad oil
1 cup hot water

Cut chicken into serving pieces.

Make a paste by blending together the next 10 ingredients. Rub paste over all surfaces of chicken pieces. Put seasoned chicken in a covered pan and marinate in the refrigerator overnight.

When ready to cook put bay leaves, cinnamon, salt, and salad oil into a Dutch oven or large skillet and heat before adding chicken pieces. Brown on all sides. Add water, cover, and simmer until chicken is tender, about 45 minutes. Serve hot or cold.

Yield: 4 to 6 servings.

TARRAGON HERBED CHICKEN

1 broiler-fryer chicken
2 teaspoons salt
4 tablespoons butter or
   margarine
2 tablespoons flour
1 cup rich chicken broth
   or 1 chicken bouillon
   cube
1¼ cups hot water

½ cup finely chopped
   onion
1 clove garlic, crushed
1 teaspoon tarragon
   leaves
¼ teaspoon ground white
   pepper
¾ cup sour cream

Wash chicken and cut into serving pieces. Add salt and rub it into chicken. Brown a few pieces at a time in butter or margarine in a Dutch oven or a heavy 10-inch skillet.

Blend flour with the pan drippings. Stir in rich chicken broth or bouillon cube, water, onion, and garlic. Cover and simmer 25 minutes. Add tarragon and ground white pepper and cook 5 minutes. Stir in sour cream. Heat only until cream is hot. DO NOT BOIL. Add additional salt and white pepper if needed.

Yield: 3 to 4 servings.

SUNDAY CHICKEN

1 broiler-fryer chicken
3 tablespoons shortening
½ cup dry white wine
   or ½ cup water and
   1 chicken bouillon
   cube
1½ teaspoons salt

¼ teaspoon ground black
   pepper
1 clove garlic, crushed
1 tablespoon flour
2 tablespoons butter or
   margarine
¼ cup grated Parmesan
   cheese

Wash, dry, and cut chicken into quarters. Brown on both sides in shortening, adding it as needed. Add wine or water and bouillon cube.

Combine salt, black pepper, and garlic. Sprinkle over chicken. Cover tightly and simmer 1 hour, or until chicken is tender.

Transfer chicken to a buttered, heatproof platter, or to a 13×9×2-inch baking dish.

Blend flour with butter or margarine and mix with pan drippings. Stir and cook ½ minute. Pour over chicken. Sprinkle with Parmesan cheese. Bake in a 350°F. oven 10 to 15 minutes, or until browned.

Serve hot with rice or new potatoes.

Yield: 4 servings.

SAGE CHICKEN WITH POLENTA

1 4-pound fricassee chicken
2 teaspoons salt
¼ teaspoon ground black pepper
¼ cup salad oil or shortening
2½ cups (1 pound 4 ounces) canned tomatoes
1 6-ounce can tomato paste
½ teaspoon ground sage
1 teaspoon salt
⅛ teaspoon ground black pepper
2 cloves garlic, crushed
¼ cup instant minced onion
1 cup yellow cornmeal
1½ teaspoons salt
1 quart boiling water

Cut chicken into serving pieces and sprinkle with the 2 teaspoons salt and ¼ teaspoon ground black pepper. Brown in hot oil or shortening. Add tomatoes, tomato paste, seasonings, and instant minced onion. Cover and simmer 50 minutes, or until chicken is tender.

Sprinkle cornmeal and salt in boiling water in top of double boiler. Bring to a rapid boil and stir and cook 10 minutes. Place over hot water. Cover and cook 30 minutes.

Turn cornmeal out on a large platter. Arrange chicken over the top over which spoon the tomato gravy. Serve hot.

Yield: 6 servings.

MARINATED CHICKEN LEGS
AND PORK IN CASSEROLE

8 chicken legs	1 small bay leaf
1 pound lean pork	1 teaspoon crushed whole
1 cup canned tomatoes	black pepper
6 sliced stuffed olives	2 cloves garlic, crushed
¼ cup finely chopped	3 teaspoons salt
onion	1 cup rice
2 tablespoons cider	
vinegar	

Place chicken legs in a 13×9×2-inch pan. Cut pork into 1-inch strips and add to chicken. Combine remaining ingredients and pour over the top. Cover and marinate 3 to 4 hours.

Cook, covered, in a 350°F. oven 1½ hours, or until chicken and pork are tender and the rice has absorbed most of the liquid.

Serve hot.

Yield: 8 servings.

FRIED CHICKEN LIVERS IN HOT SAUCE

¾ *cup chicken livers, cut*   ½ *teaspoon red pepper*
    into small pieces   1 *tablespoon dark brown*
2 *tablespoons olive oil*   *sugar*
1 *cup finely chopped*   1 *teaspoon lime juice*
    onion   1 *bay leaf*
1 *clove garlic, grated*   ¾ *cup* COCONUT WATER

Sauté chicken livers in oil until nicely browned; add onion, garlic; continue cooking 5 minutes. Add red pepper, brown sugar, lime juice, bay leaf, COCONUT WATER; blend well. Simmer 15 to 20 minutes, or until chicken liver is done.

Yield: 2 servings.

EAST INDIAN FRIED CHICKEN

2 2½*-pound chickens*   2 *tablespoons brown*
2 *tablespoons salt*   *sugar*
1 *teaspoon pepper*   1 *teaspoon lime juice*
½ *teaspoon garlic salt*   1 *teaspoon curry powder*
¼ *cup olive oil*   3 *tablespoons olive oil*
2 *small onions*   1 *cup* COCONUT WATER
2 *cloves garlic*   2 *bay leaves*

Wash and dry chickens; cut into serving pieces.

Combine salt, pepper, and garlic salt and rub into chicken pieces. Brown chicken in olive oil; set aside.

Grind together onions and garlic; add brown sugar, lime juice, curry powder; fry 5 to 10 minutes in the 3 tablespoons olive oil. Add COCONUT WATER, bay leaves; pour over browned chicken. Simmer about 30 minutes, or until chicken is tender, sauce is thick.

Yield: 6 to 8 servings.

SMOTHERED TURKEY

7 *cloves garlic*	10 *small whole onions,*
¾ *teaspoon ground pepper*	*peeled*
or 12 peppercorns	4 *bay leaves*
5 *teaspoons oregano*	12 *green olives, pitted*
10 *teaspoons salt*	12 *tablespoons capers*
2 *tablespoons vinegar*	1 *tablespoon liquid from*
1 *8½-pound turkey, cut*	*jar of capers*
into serving pieces	½ *cup white wine*
12 *dry prunes, pitted*	¾ *cup sugar*

Grind garlic, pepper or peppercorns, oregano, salt together; add vinegar; rub into turkey pieces.

Place turkey giblets in Dutch oven. Add turkey pieces. Place prunes, onions, bay leaves, olives, capers, caper juice on top of turkey pieces. Cover; place in refrigerator overnight. Next day, cook over medium heat 10 minutes; reduce heat to low; cook 2 hours. Add wine, sugar; simmer 1 hour longer.

Yield: 8 servings.

RICE WITH DUCK

1 *4- to 5-pound duck*	½ *teaspoon ground*
2 *tablespoons butter or*	*marjoram*
margarine	2 *cloves garlic, crushed*
3 *cups boiling water*	¹⁄₁₆ *teaspoon ground red*
1 *tablespoon salt*	*pepper*
1 *cup finely chopped*	1 *cup uncooked,*
onion	*long-grain rice*
2 *teaspoons ground*	
cumin seed	

Remove excess fat from duck and cut duck into 4 pieces. Brown in a Dutch oven or heavy deep skillet in butter or margarine. Add 1 cup of the water and salt. Cover and cook 45 minutes, or until tender. Skim off excess fat. Add spices and remaining water. Mix well. Add rice. Cover and cook 20 minutes, or until tender. Serve hot.

Yield: 4 servings.

CHINESE ROAST DUCK

1 6- or 7-pound lean duck

2 teaspoons minced green onion tops

2 or 3 cloves garlic, finely minced

1 tablespoon ready-made brown bean sauce

1 teaspoon Ac'cent

1 teaspoon ground cinnamon

1 tablespoon brown sugar

1 seed of star anise, crushed (optional)

2 teaspoons rice wine or sherry

⅛ teaspoon white pepper

1¼ teaspoons salt

1 can chicken stock or water

1 tablespoon honey

1½ tablespoons soy bean sauce

1 tablespoon cold water

Scald dressed duck with boiling water two or three times, drain and dry.

Mix all ingredients except the stock, honey, and soy bean sauce. When thoroughly mixed, stir in the stock or water, bring to a boil, allow to boil up 1 minute. Tie duck at neck with string and pour in the hot mixture, which will be extremely liquid. Sew up opening and rub entire surface of duck with mixture of the honey, soy bean sauce, and tablespoon of cold water. Roast in a 425°F. to 450°F. oven 40 to

50 minutes. Baste with liquid accumulated in pan. Uncover, turn on all sides to get bird brown and crisp.

Yield: 4 servings.

CHRISTMAS DUCK

1 4- to 5-pound duck
1 cup white wine
3 tablespoons fresh
   lemon juice
1 tablespoon parsley
   flakes
2 tablespoons finely
   chopped onion
2 cloves garlic, crushed
2½ teaspoons salt or salt
   to taste

Duck giblets
1 tablespoon melted
   butter or margarine
½ teaspoon ground
   nutmeg
¼ teaspoon ground black
   pepper
1 11-ounce can
   water-packed
   chestnuts

Wash duck and wipe dry.

Combine wine, lemon juice, parsley flakes, onion, garlic, and 1 teaspoon of the salt. Pour over duck. Marinate overnight.

Wash giblets and chop coarsely. Add melted butter or margarine, nutmeg, ground black pepper, and remaining 1½ teaspoons salt.

Chop chestnuts and add. Mix well and spoon into body and neck cavities of the duck. Close openings with skewers. Lace tightly with a string. Place on a rack in a roasting pan. Bake in moderate oven (325°F.) 2 to 2¼ hours, or until duck is tender and skin is brown and crisp.

Yield: 4 servings.

DUCK JAMBALAYA

*1 4-pound ready-to-cook
   duck*
3½ teaspoons salt
*¾ teaspoon ground black
   pepper*
2 cups GIBLET STOCK
1 cup long-grain rice
¼ cup sweet pepper flakes
¼ cup water
½ pound sausage
*1 cup finely chopped
   onion*

2 cloves garlic, crushed
1 medium-size bay leaf
½ teaspoon chili powder
½ teaspoon ground thyme
1 teaspoon parsley flakes
*½ cup diced cooked
   giblets*
*½ cup diced cooked
   ham*
1 cup canned tomatoes

Wash duck, cut into quarters, and trim off excess fat and
bone. (Discard fat, but save bones to cook with giblets.)
Mix 2 teaspoons of the salt with ½ teaspoon of the black
pepper and rub into duck. Brown 2 pieces of duck at a time,
very slowly, in a 4-quart saucepan, 30 to 40 minutes each.
As duck browns, place it on paper towels to absorb fat. Pour
off excess fat from saucepan and stir in GIBLET STOCK. Add
browned duck, cover, and cook slowly 1½ hours, or until
it is tender.

Soak rice in cold water to cover at least 30 minutes. Drain
well.

In the meantime, soften sweet pepper flakes in the ¼
cup water. Set aside for later use.

Brown sausage and drain off excess fat and discard it.
Add rice, onion, sweet pepper flakes, and garlic and stir and
cook with sausage until rice is dry and sticks to bottom of
pan.

Remove duck from pan. Stir rice mixture into gravy. Add
remaining salt and black pepper along with bay leaf, chili
powder, thyme, and parsley flakes. Toss lightly with a fork to

mix well. Cover and cook 10 minutes, or until almost tender. Add diced duck giblets, ham, and tomatoes. Mix, being careful not to mash rice. Place duck on top of rice. Cover and cook 10 minutes. Serve rice, topped with a serving of duck.

Yield: 4 servings.

GIBLET STOCK:

Wash giblets and place neck, gizzard, and bones in a saucepan with 1 quart water and ½ teaspoon salt. Cover and cook 30 to 40 minutes, or until giblets are tender. Add liver 10 minutes before cooking time is up.

DUCK STUFFED WITH
PINEAPPLE AND PEANUTS

1 6-pound duck	*1 tablespoon grated*
1 clove garlic, crushed	*onion*
1 teaspoon salt	*¼ teaspoon ginger*
Dash pepper	*½ cup orange juice*
1 teaspoon onion juice	*½ cup fresh pineapple*
¾ cup bread crumbs	*juice*
¾ cup ground peanuts	*2 tablespoons flour*
¾ cup chopped fresh	*1 cup water*
pineapple	*¼ cup sliced olives*
¾ cup sour cream	*(optional)*

Wipe duck with damp cloth. Rub with garlic, salt, pepper, and onion juice. Combine bread crumbs, peanuts, pineapple, sour cream, onion, and ginger; stuff lightly into duck. Close opening with skewers or sew together and truss. Place on rack in shallow roasting pan and place in 450°F. oven 30 minutes, or until lightly browned. Reduce heat to 325°F. and continue roasting 1½ hours. Combine orange and pineapple juice and baste duck several times with the mixture.

Remove duck to hot platter, pour off most of the fat, add flour to remaining fat, stir to a paste, add water, and stir until smooth and thickened. Add olives, if desired, and continue cooking 5 minutes.

Yield: 4 to 6 servings.

Seafoods

Eat no onions nor garlic, for we are to utter sweet breath.

—*A Midsummer Night's Dream, Shakespeare*

SPANISH CODFISH, COUNTRY STYLE

1 pound salt codfish	1 3- or 4-ounce can
2 cloves garlic	pimientos
⅓ cup oil	1 egg, beaten
1 pound tomatoes or	Salt and pepper
1¼ cups canned	
tomatoes	

Soak codfish overnight in cold water to cover.

Brown garlic in very hot oil and remove. To the oil add chopped peeled tomatoes, pimientos cut in strips, and codfish. Cook, covered, about 20 minutes. When ready to serve, stir in well-beaten egg; season. Serve at once.

Yield: 6 servings.

BACALHAO

1 pound salt codfish	Salt to taste
1 onion, sliced	⅛ teaspoon pepper
1 clove garlic, split	¼ teaspoon cumin
1 tablespoon oil	seed
2½ cups tomatoes	
1 tablespoon minced	
parsley	

Soak codfish in water for five minutes, drain, and repeat twice, then flake the fish.

Sauté onion and garlic in oil until tender but not browned. Add tomatoes, seasonings, and fish. Cover and simmer 15 minutes, or until codfish is tender.

Yield: 4 servings.

BOUILLABAISSE

*1 pound sea bass, cut
into ½-inch slices
1 pound red snapper,
cut into ½-inch
slices
1 pound eels, cut into
½-inch slices
1 pound halibut, cut
into ½-inch slices
1 pound cod, cut into
½-inch slices
1 pound raw shrimp,
cleaned and deveined*

*2 medium-size lobsters,
cleaned
½ cup olive oil
¾ cup chopped onion
2 tomatoes, peeled
4 cloves garlic, crushed
1 tablespoon chopped
parsley
Pinch saffron
Pinch thyme
1 bay leaf
Cold water
Salt and pepper
Sliced French bread*

Place all ingredients, except bread, in large kettle. Cook over high heat so that it comes to a boil rapidly. Cook quickly, only 12 to 15 minutes.

Place slices of bread on bottom of large soup bowls and pour liquid over, dividing fish among all the plates.

Yield: 6 to 8 servings.

FISH KEBABS IN GARLIC MARINADE

*¼ cup salad oil
¼ cup cider vinegar
1 tablespoon sweet
pepper flakes
1 teaspoon garlic salt
½ teaspoon onion salt
½ teaspoon salt*

*½ teaspoon thyme leaves,
crushed
½ teaspoon basil leaves,
crushed
½ teaspoon coarse ground
black pepper
1½ pounds fish steaks,
cut into 1-inch cubes*

In a small saucepan or skillet combine all ingredients except fish. Cook over very low heat for about 10 minutes to blend flavors.

Pour over fish as a marinade. Refrigerate and let stand 4 to 5 hours or overnight.

String fish on skewers to broil. Or, alternate fish bits with quick-cooking vegetables, i.e. pieces of tomatoes, mushrooms, or eggplant. Brush with marinade and broil over hot coals for about 5 minutes, turning to brown evenly.

Yield: 6 servings.

GRILLED SWORDFISH

1¼ to 1½ pounds swordfish steaks	*1 or 2 cloves garlic, crushed*
1 small onion, minced	*1 teaspoon salt*
1 tablespoon minced parsley	*½ cup olive oil*
	¼ cup lemon juice

Have the swordfish sliced as thin as possible. Place in a large deep bowl and cover with marinade consisting of onion, parsley, garlic, salt, ¼ cup of the olive oil and 1 tablespoon lemon juice; leave in marinade several hours at room temperature.

When ready to cook, preheat broiler oven, then lay marinated swordfish slices on foil-lined broiler pan and place 4 inches from heat. Cook 7 to 10 minutes, until lightly browned; turn, cook on the other side for about 5 minutes. Fish should flake easily.

Yield: 4 servings.

Pass a sauce consisting of remaining ¼ cup olive oil and 3 tablespoons lemon juice, to be spooned over servings of fish at table.

FISH IN GARLIC BARBECUE SAUCE

¼ cup fresh lemon juice
¼ cup cider vinegar
1 teaspoon salt
1 teaspoon garlic salt
1 teaspoon paprika
1 teaspoon powdered
  mustard

½ teaspoon ground black
  pepper
⅛ teaspoon ground red
  pepper
2 pounds fish steaks
  (*halibut, cod, salmon*)

Combine all ingredients except fish in a small saucepan.
Heat to boiling. Cool. Brush fish with sauce when broiling;
baste often. If desired, turn fish and broil second side, brushing on sauce.

Most fish broils to flaky tenderness in about 10 minutes
total time.

Yield: 4 to 6 servings; ½ cup sauce.

PAELLA

⅔ cup olive oil
4 cloves garlic, mashed
1 cup minced onion
½ cup chopped sweet
  red pepper
2 bay leaves
Dash saffron
1 cup diced, uncooked
  chicken
½ cup diced, cooked
  lobster
1 cup flaked, cooked
  pompano or red
  snapper

½ cup chopped, cooked
  shrimp
¾ cup chopped, cooked
  clams
1 cup uncooked regular
  rice
1½ cups boiling water
1 cup uncooked green
  peas
2 teaspoons salt
Dash pepper
½ cup sherry wine

Sauté in ⅓ cup olive oil the garlic, onion, red pepper, bay leaves, saffron; add chicken; cook 15 to 20 minutes. Add lobster, pompano or snapper, shrimp, clams. Add rice to remaining ⅓ cup olive oil; fry until light brown. Add fish mixture, water, peas, salt, pepper; simmer 15 minutes, or until rice is cooked. Place in a 350°F. oven 20 minutes, or until dry. Remove from oven; let stand 10 minutes; add sherry. Garnish with hard-cooked egg slices, strips sweet red pepper. *Yield:* 6 servings.

SHRIMP IN TOMATO AND GINGER SAUCE

½ cup olive oil
1 teaspoon ground ginger
2 cloves garlic, minced

½ cup ketchup
2 pounds cleaned, cooked shrimp

Combine olive oil, ground ginger, and garlic in fry pan; simmer 4 minutes. Add ketchup; mix well. Add shrimp; toss lightly; cover; simmer 10 minutes. *Yield:* 4 servings.

FRIED SHRIMP IN HOT SAUCE

1 cup finely chopped
  onions
1 clove garlic, grated
2 tablespoons olive oil
½ teaspoon red pepper
1 tablespoon dark
  brown sugar

1 teaspoon lime juice
¾ cup raw, cleaned,
  deveined shrimp,
  cut into ½-inch pieces
2 bay leaves
1 cup COCONUT WATER

Sauté onions and garlic in olive oil; add red pepper, brown sugar, lime juice; blend well. Add shrimp, bay leaves; continue cooking 5 minutes. Add COCONUT WATER; simmer 20 minutes, or until shrimp is done.

Yield: 2 servings.

SCAMPI

½ pound (2 sticks) butter or margarine	6 cloves garlic, crushed
¼ cup olive oil	¾ teaspoon salt
1 tablespoon parsley flakes	1 tablespoon fresh lemon juice
¾ teaspoon basil leaves	1 pound large fresh shrimp
½ teaspoon oregano leaves	

Melt butter or margarine. Add olive oil, parsley flakes, basil leaves, oregano leaves, garlic, salt, lemon juice.

Peel and devein uncooked shrimp, leaving tails attached. Split down the inside lengthwise center, being careful not to cut through the shrimp. Spread open to simulate butterflies. Place in a shallow baking pan, tail end up. Pour sauce over all. Bake in a preheated very hot oven (450°F.) 5 minutes. Place under broiler 5 minutes to brown.

Yield: 6 servings.

STUFFED PATTIES

¼ cup minced onion	1 teaspoon salt
2 cloves garlic, finely grated	½ pound cooked, cleaned shrimp
2 tablespoons butter or margarine	1 10-ounce package pie crust mix
½ teaspoon pepper	Oil

Sauté onion and garlic in butter or margarine until golden brown; add pepper, salt.

Cut cooked shrimp into ½-inch pieces; add to onion mixture; blend well; cool.

Prepare pastry dough; divide in half. Roll each piece of dough into circle ⅛ inch thick; cut into 6 or 7 equal pieces. Divide shrimp mixture in half; spoon onto one end of each piece of dough. Wet edges of dough; fold dough over shrimp mixture; seal edges.

Pour oil into fry pan to depth of ¼ inch; heat to 375°F. Fry shrimp patties in hot oil until golden brown, about 3 minutes on each side. Place on paper towels to drain.

Yield: 12 to 14 medium-size patties.

CLAMS D'ALESSIO

¼ *cup butter*
2 *8-ounce cans minced clams*
2 *teaspoons cornstarch in 2 tablespoons water*
¼ *cup dry white wine*
4 *cloves garlic, crushed*
1 *tablespoon finely chopped onion*
⅛ *teaspoon basil*
⅛ *teaspoon oregano*
⅛ *teaspoon white pepper*
1 *2-ounce can mushroom pieces*
5 *cups water*
¼ *teaspoon salt*
1 *12-ounce package spaghetti*
Grated Parmesan cheese

Melt butter in frying pan, add undrained clams, cornstarch, wine, seasonings, and undrained mushrooms. Simmer 20 minutes, stirring occasionally.

Meanwhile, bring water and salt to a boil, add spaghetti,

and cook until done. Drain and rinse spaghetti in hot water. Arrange spaghetti on plates, pour clam sauce over all, and sprinkle with Parmesan cheese. Serve very hot.

Yield: 6 servings.

FROGS' LEGS NICOISE

24 small or medium	*6 tomatoes, peeled*
frogs' legs	*6 cloves garlic, minced*
Flour	*Chopped parsley*
1¼ cups olive oil	*Juice of 1 lemon*
¾ pound butter	

Remove feet and black part from top of frogs' legs. Soak in cold water 2 hours. Remove frogs' legs from water and dry. Dust with flour. Heat 1 cup oil and half the butter in large skillet. Place frogs' legs in hot oil and butter and simmer about 5 minutes on each side, or until brown. Remove from skillet and keep warm.

Cut tomatoes in half. Squeeze out juice and dice.

Sauté 1 minced clove garlic in remaining ¼ cup oil. Add diced tomatoes. Cook 10 to 15 minutes.

Melt remaining butter in another skillet. Add remaining garlic and brown slightly. Place frogs' legs on a platter with tomatoes in center. Sprinkle with parsley and lemon juice. Pour garlic butter mixture over before serving.

Yield: 4 servings.

LOBSTER CREOLE

2 medium-size onions,
  chopped
2 large green peppers,
  chopped
2 cloves garlic, minced
½ cup olive oil
1½ teaspoons salt
¼ teaspoon pepper

2 medium-size fresh
  tomatoes, peeled,
  cored, and quartered
2 pounds cooked lobster
  meat, cut into small
  pieces
2 8-ounce cans tomato
  sauce
½ cup white cooking
  wine

Sauté onions, green peppers, and garlic in olive oil until tender. Add salt and pepper. Add fresh tomatoes; cook until soft. Stir lobster meat in tomato sauce; simmer 15 minutes. Add white wine; cook 2 to 3 minutes longer.

Serve over cooked rice. Garnish with pickled red peppers.

Yield: 6 servings.

ESCARGOTS

1¼ cups butter
1 tablespoon chopped
  shallots
4 cloves garlic, crushed
2 teaspoons chopped
  parsley

¾ teaspoon salt
Pepper to taste
50 canned snails and
  shells
Bread crumbs
Melted butter

Cream together butter, shallots, garlic, parsley, salt, and pepper to taste.

Place snails in shells and fill each shell with garlic butter. Sprinkle bread crumbs over snails. Sprinkle melted butter on crumbs. Bake in a 400°F. oven or under broiler for about 10 minutes, or until piping hot.

Yield: 4 servings.

LOBSTER FRA DIAVALO

2 1½-pound lobsters, washed and claws removed
¼ cup olive oil
2 cloves garlic, minced
⅛ teaspoon salt
⅛ teaspoon pepper
2 tablespoons finely chopped onion

1 pound tomatoes, peeled and chopped
1 cup white wine
1 teaspoon oregano
2 tablespoons chopped parsley
½ teaspoon crushed red pepper seeds

Cut each lobster into 3 pieces and crack claws.

Heat oil in Dutch oven. When oil is hot, add lobsters and cook for 3 to 4 minutes. Add garlic, stir. Add salt, pepper, and onion. Cook 2 minutes. Add remaining ingredients when lobster is red. Continue cooking over high heat for 10 minutes.

Yield: 2 servings.

PETONCLES PROVENCALE

(Scallops of Provence)

3 cups scallops
¾ cup olive oil
1 large clove garlic, minced

1 cup sliced mushroom caps
1 cup soft bread crumbs

Chop scallops coarsely.

Heat ½ cup of the olive oil in a skillet. Add scallops and garlic and cook, stirring constantly, until lightly browned.

Heat 2 tablespoons of the remaining oil in another skillet; add mushrooms and cook, stirring occasionally, for 5 minutes.

Brown bread crumbs in remaining 2 tablespoons oil.

Drain scallops and mushrooms; combine and place on serving platter. Sprinkle with crumbs. Garnish with deep-fat fried parsley and serve with AIOLI SAUCE.

Yield: 4 servings.

Vegetables

Our apothecary's shop is our garden full of pot herbs, and our doctor is a clove of garlic.

—*A Deep Snow, 1615*

PEPPERS IN OIL

3 large red peppers   Salt to taste
¾ cup pitted black olives   Olive oil
2 cloves garlic, crushed

Roast the peppers in a hot skillet, turning so as not to pierce skin. Remove skin from peppers and discard. Cut peppers into strips and combine with olives, garlic, and salt. Marinate in olive oil. Remove peppers and olives from olive oil when ready to serve.

Yield: 6 servings.

RATATOUILLE

Olive oil   3 cloves garlic, crushed
1 pound eggplant, peeled   1 onion, sliced
   and sliced   Bouquet garni (parsley,
½ pound squash,   thyme, bay leaf, and
   peeled and sliced   2 cloves tied in small
½ pound green peppers,   sack)
   sliced   ½ teaspoon tarragon
1 pound tomatoes,   Salt and pepper to taste
   quartered

Heat oil in large skillet. Lightly sauté eggplant, squash, and green peppers until tender. Add tomatoes, garlic, onion, bouquet garni, tarragon, and salt and pepper to taste. Cover and simmer for 1 hour. Remove bouquet garni before serving.

Yield: 6 servings.

SOFRITO EGGPLANT

1½ slices bacon, diced
3 tablespoons finely
　chopped ham
⅓ cup chopped onion
¼ teaspoon chopped
　garlic
3 tablespoons finely
　chopped tomato
2 tablespoons finely
　chopped green peppers
5 cups (1½ pounds)
　peeled and diced
　eggplant

1 tablespoon chopped
　green olives
¼ teaspoon chopped
　capers
¾ teaspoon oregano
　leaves
⅛ teaspoon ground black
　pepper
½ cup water

Fry bacon and ham together until crisp. Add next 4 ingredients. Stir and cook 5 minutes over low heat. Add eggplant along with remaining ingredients. Cover and cook 7 to 8 minutes, or until done, over low heat. Serve hot as a vegetable.

Yield: 6 servings.

EGGPLANT, TURKISH STYLE

5 pounds (about 4
  medium) eggplant
¾ cup salad oil
3 teaspoons fresh lemon
  juice
6 tablespoons hot water
½ cup flour
3 tablespoons finely
  chopped onion
1 clove garlic, minced
½ cup chopped fresh
  mushrooms

1 tablespoon butter or
  margarine
2 tablespoons minced
  fresh parsley
1½ cups (2 medium)
  diced fresh tomatoes
1 cup ground or diced
  cooked lamb
4 teaspoons salt
½ teaspoon ground black
  pepper
2 eggs, slightly beaten

Wash eggplants and cut 3 of them in half lengthwise. Run a sharp-pointed stainless steel knife around the inside of the skins, separating the sides from the skins. Score pulp deeply, cutting almost through, being careful not to pierce the skin.

Pour 2 tablespoons of the oil into a 9- or 10-inch skillet. Heat. Place 2 eggplant halves at a time, cut side down, and cook 1 minute.

Combine 1 teaspoon lemon juice and 2 tablespoons hot water and add. Cover and cook over medium heat 10 minutes. Remove from pan and scoop out the pulp, leaving the skins intact. (Place pulp in a bowl and save for use later.) Repeat, using the remaining 4 eggplant halves.

Cut the whole eggplant into ½-inch slices and peel. Coat lightly with flour and brown on both sides in the rest of the oil, adding 2 tablespoons at a time.

Sauté onion, garlic, and mushrooms in butter or margarine and combine with cooked eggplant pulp. Stir in parsley, tomatoes, lamb, salt, black pepper, and eggs.

Line an oiled 2-quart charlotte mold or deep casserole with

eggplant skins, having the purple side next to the sides of the mold and extending over the sides. Place a 1-inch layer of the eggplant and lamb mixture in the bottom of the mold. Over this place a layer of fried eggplant slices. Repeat until the mold is filled, having the eggplant mixture as the last layer. Bring the skins, which extend over the side of the mold, over the top. (If skins are not long enough to completely cover top, place a piece of foil over the bare portion.) Bake in a pan of hot water in a preheated moderate oven (375°F.) 1½ hours. Remove from oven and let stand 10 minutes. Unmold onto a serving plate. Serve hot with tomato sauce. *Yield:* 8 servings.

STEWED EGGPLANT, SPANISH STYLE

1 1½-pound eggplant
1 teaspoon salt
¼ cup olive or salad oil
½ cup Spanish type
  tomato sauce
½ cup water
1 cup chopped green
  pepper
¼ cup finely chopped
  onion
5 stuffed olives, sliced
1 teaspoon oregano
  leaves

1 teaspoon capers
  (optional)
¼ teaspoon ground black
  pepper
8 cloves garlic, crushed
¹⁄₁₆ teaspoon ground red
  pepper
1 pound ground lean
  beef
1 teaspoon salt
Hot cooked rice
SPANISH STYLE BEANS

Wash, peel, and cut eggplant into ½-inch dice. Place in a bowl with 1 teaspoon salt. Add water to cover. Let stand while preparing sauce.

Heat olive or salad oil 1 to 2 minutes. Add the next 10 ingredients. Cook slowly 2 minutes. (Save out ¼ of the sauce to add to beans later.) Add meat and 1 teaspoon salt. Mix well. Simmer 5 minutes.

Drain eggplant, reserving 1 cup of the water, and add both eggplant and the 1 cup water to the sauce. Cover and cook over medium heat 30 minutes, or until eggplant is tender. Serve hot with rice and SPANISH STYLE BEANS.

Yield: 8 to 10 servings.

SPANISH STYLE BEANS:

Combine the tomato sauce, reserved for the beans, and 2 pounds canned pinto or kidney beans (undrained) and 1 teaspoon salt. Bring to a quick boil, reduce heat, and cook 20 minutes, or until the sauce has thickened. Serve as a side dish with eggplant.

EGGPLANT BRINDISI

2 slices bacon, diced
2 cups finely chopped ham
½ cup finely chopped onion
1 clove garlic, crushed
¼ cup chopped green pepper
¾ cup finely chopped tomato
1 tablespoon chopped stuffed olives
¼ teaspoon chopped capers
½ teaspoon crushed oregano leaves
½ teaspoon crushed basil leaves
¼ teaspoon salt
¼ teaspoon ground black pepper
¼ cup water
1 1½-pound eggplant
1 clove garlic, crushed
2 tablespoons Parmesan cheese
2 tablespoons olive or salad oil
6 slices Italian bread

Fry bacon and ham together until bacon is crisp. Add onion, garlic, pepper, and tomato. Stir and cook over low heat 10 minutes. Add next 7 ingredients and cook 5 minutes.

Wash, peel, and cut eggplant into ¼-inch lengthwise slices. Place in a 2-quart casserole. Spoon ham-tomato mixture over all. Cover. Bake in a preheated moderate oven (350°F.) 25 minutes. Remove cover.

Stir crushed garlic clove and cheese into olive or salad oil. Spread on bread slices. Place spread side up on top of eggplant and continue baking 20 minutes, or until bread is lightly browned.

Yield: 6 servings.

AUBERGINES AU FOUR

(Oven-baked Eggplant)

6 small eggplants
½ cup butter or
  margarine
6 large tomatoes, cut
  into eighths
2 cloves garlic, crushed
Salt and pepper to taste

½ cup chicken or veal
  stock
½ cup buttered bread
  crumbs
½ cup grated Parmesan
  cheese

Pare eggplants; cut pulp into strips.

Melt butter or margarine in a deep kettle; add eggplant, tomatoes, and garlic. Sauté about 10 minutes, stirring occasionally. Season to taste with salt and pepper. Place mixture into a large, buttered casserole; add chicken or veal stock and cover. Bake in a 275°F. oven 2 hours, adding additional stock if necessary.

Combine bread crumbs and cheese. Uncover casserole; sprinkle crumb mixture over top. Place under broiler until lightly browned.

Yield: 12 servings.

CHAMPIGNONS A LA POULETTE EN CAISSE

(Stuffed Mushroom Rolls)

3 cups mushrooms
5 tablespoons butter
3 cups chicken bouillon
2 tablespoons flour
3 egg yolks, slightly
  beaten

6 large rolls
Garlic butter (see note)
2 tablespoons minced
  parsley
2 tablespoons chives

Remove stems from mushrooms; measure 1 cup of the stems.

Melt 3 tablespoons of the butter in a skillet; add mushroom caps and cook until tender, stirring occasionally, reserve.

Add mushroom stems to boiling chicken bouillon in a saucepan. Remove from heat and let steep until lukewarm. Strain into another saucepan and boil rapidly until liquid is reduced to 2 cups. Melt remaining 2 tablespoons butter in a saucepan; blend in flour. Gradually add mushroom stock and cook, stirring constantly, until mixture thickens and comes to a boil. Remove from heat. Add egg yolks, stirring rapidly. Return to low heat and cook, stirring constantly, until thickened. Stir in mushroom caps; heat.

Cut a slice from the top of each roll; carefully remove insides without breaking the walls. Brush outsides with melted garlic butter. Bake in a 375°F. oven until golden. Spoon in mushroom mixture. Sprinkle with parsley and chives.

Yield: 6 servings.

NOTE: To make garlic butter allow 1 clove garlic, crushed, to 1 tablespoon butter. Blend garlic and butter in mortar or small bowl.

FUNGHI ALLA PARMIGIANA
(Cheese-Stuffed Mushrooms)

2 *pounds large*	2 *cloves garlic, diced*
mushrooms	3 *tablespoons diced*
½ *cup grated Parmesan*	*parsley*
cheese	*Salt and pepper*
¾ *cup dry bread crumbs*	½ *teaspoon oregano*
1 *cup grated onions*	¾ *cup olive oil*

Wash mushrooms, remove stems, and chop.

Mix in cheese, bread crumbs, onions, garlic, parsley, salt, pepper, and oregano. Place this mixture into mushroom caps. Pour ½ cup oil into baking pan and place mushrooms in pan. Pour remaining oil over each mushroom. Bake in a 350°F. oven about 25 minutes.

Yield: 6 to 8 servings.

Salads and Salad Dressings

The Romans believed garlic to be an aphrodisiac.

CAESAR SALAD

4 cloves garlic, crushed
1 cup olive oil
3 quarts salad greens
½ cup salad oil
½ cup grated Parmesan
  cheese
¼ cup Roquefort cheese
1 tablespoon
  Worcestershire sauce

½ teaspoon powdered
  mustard
Salt and pepper to taste
1 raw egg
¼ cup fresh lemon juice
2 cups crisp croutons

Add garlic to olive oil and allow to stand several hours at room temperature. Place salad greens in large bowl and pour over salad oil, Parmesan cheese, Roquefort cheese, Worcestershire sauce, powdered mustard, salt and pepper to taste. Mix well. Break raw egg over greens and pour in lemon juice. Toss thoroughly so that greens are coated with egg, seasonings, and cheese. Dip croutons in garlic-flavored oil, allowing croutons to soak. Toss croutons into salad, leaving remaining garlic-flavored olive oil aside.

Yield: 8 servings.

GUACAMOLE SALAD

1 ripe avocado, well
  mashed
1 pimiento, chopped
2 tablespoons finely
  chopped onion

1 clove garlic, crushed
1 large tomato, peeled
  and finely chopped
Salt and pepper to taste

Combine all ingredients. Mix well and chill until ready to serve. This cannot be made too far ahead of time as the avocado will turn dark. A little lemon juice squeezed on the avocado will help to prevent this.

Yield: 2 cups.

CREAMY GARLIC DRESSING

1 teaspoon powdered mustard	2 teaspoons sugar
2 teaspoons water	¼ teaspoon ground black pepper
1 teaspoon salt	1 clove garlic, crushed
1 teaspoon paprika	¼ cup cider vinegar
1 teaspoon celery seed	½ cup salad oil

Mix mustard and water and let stand 10 minutes to develop flavor. Place in the top of a double boiler along with salt, paprika, celery seed, sugar, black pepper, garlic, and vinegar. Heat over hot water (not boiling). Gradually beat in the oil. Cool and refrigerate.

Yield: ¾ cup.

ONION SALAD DRESSING

1½ teaspoons powdered mustard	½ teaspoon ground black pepper
1 tablespoon water	1 clove garlic, crushed
1¾ teaspoons salt	¼ cup finely chopped onion
1 teaspoon sugar	1 cup salad oil
1 teaspoon paprika	¼ cup cider vinegar
½ teaspoon celery seed	

Blend mustard with water and let stand 10 minutes to develop flavor. Add salt, sugar, paprika, celery seed, black pepper, garlic, onion, and oil. Let stand 1 hour. Add vinegar and beat about ½ minute with a rotary beater.

Yield: 1⅓ cups.

MEXICALI DRESSING

1 hard-cooked egg yolk	½ teaspoon chili powder
¾ cup French dressing	1 clove garlic, crushed
1½ tablespoons	
Worcestershire sauce	

Sieve the egg yolk into the French dressing.

Blend the Worcestershire sauce, chili powder, and garlic together and stir into dressing. This dressing is best made several hours in advance so it will have time to "ripen."

Yield: ¾ cup.

AVOCADO DRESSING

½ medium-ripe avocado	4 gloves garlic, crushed
½ cup mayonnaise	⅛ teaspoon salt
1 tablespoon lemon juice	Dash ground red pepper
½ teaspoon	
Worcestershire sauce	

In mixing bowl mash avocado with a fork; stir in mayonnaise, lemon juice, and seasonings. Serve over lettuce.

This may also be used as a dip for chips or as a spread for thin crackers.

Yield: ¾ cup.

BLACK PEPPER TOMATO
SALAD DRESSING

*1 cup diced fresh
tomatoes
½ teaspoon salt
¼ teaspoon ground black
pepper*

*2 tablespoons finely
chopped onion
½ clove garlic, crushed
3 tablespoons salad oil
2 tablespoons wine
vinegar*

Mash tomatoes and put through a sieve. Add salt, black pepper, onion, garlic, salad oil, and vinegar. Beat with a rotary beater. Or, if desired, put all ingredients in an electric blender and blend ½ minute. Serve over salad greens or other fresh vegetable salads.

Yield: Approximately 1 cup.

HERBED FRENCH DRESSING

*3 teaspoons salt
1 teaspoon oregano
leaves
1 teaspoon basil leaves
1 teaspoon tarragon
leaves
2 tablespoons finely
chopped onion
½ teaspoon sugar*

*4 cloves garlic, crushed
½ teaspoon powdered
mustard
⅛ teaspoon ground
black pepper
1 cup salad oil
¼ cup cider vinegar
5 tablespoons lemon
juice*

Combine first 10 ingredients. Let stand at least 1 hour. Add vinegar and lemon juice. Beat well with rotary beater.

Yield: 1⅓ cups.

GARLIC FRENCH DRESSING

*1½ teaspoons powdered
   mustard*
1 tablespoon water
1½ teaspoons salt
*1½ teaspoons instant
   minced onion*
1 teaspoon sugar
1 teaspoon paprika

*¼ teaspoon ground black
   pepper*
2 cloves garlic, crushed
1 cup olive or salad oil
*¼ cup cider or wine
   vinegar*
*1 tablespoon fresh
   lemon juice*

Mix mustard with water and let stand 10 minutes to develop flavor. Mix with the next 7 ingredients and let stand 1 hour. Add vinegar and lemon juice. Beat with a rotary beater or in a blender until slightly thick and creamy. Serve on vegetable salads. *Yield:* Approximately 1⅓ cups.

CREAMY FRENCH DRESSING

1 small clove garlic
1½ teaspoons salt
⅔ cup salad oil
⅓ cup vinegar

⅓ cup heavy cream
*Pepper to taste, red
   pepper if you can
   take it*

Cut garlic into pieces on a chopping board and sprinkle with the salt. Mash the salt and garlic together with the flat side of a knife blade. Continue rubbing the garlic until it is completely blended with the salt. Combine the garlic salt with the remaining ingredients. The dressing is best allowed to "ripen" for several hours before serving. Stir well or shake just before serving on wedges of iceberg lettuce.

Yield: 1⅓ cups.

SORRENTO TOMATO DRESSING

2 ½-inch slices fresh
  white bread
2 cloves garlic
1 8-ounce can tomato
  sauce
1½ teaspoons salt

1 teaspoon sugar
½ teaspoon paprika
¼ teaspoon pepper
⅓ cup salad oil
¼ cup cider vinegar

Remove bread crusts.

Cut garlic in thin slices and insert in bread. Let stand 1 hour; remove garlic. Crumble bread into small bowl and add tomato sauce, salt, sugar, paprika, and pepper. Beat in salad oil and vinegar. Cover. Chill well. Stir before serving. Serve on simple green salads.

Yield: Approximately 1½ cups.

SPECIAL ROQUEFORT DRESSING

¼ pound Roquefort
  cheese
⅓ cup heavy cream or
  undiluted evaporated
  milk
½ cup mayonnaise
⅓ cup salad oil

⅓ cup red wine vinegar
1 clove garlic, chopped
½ teaspoon
  Worcestershire sauce
Generous dash of salt
¼ teaspoon coarse black
  pepper

Have cheese at room temperature. Place cheese in a small mixing bowl; mash well with a fork. Gradually beat in cream, then mayonnaise, oil, and vinegar. Add remaining ingredients, blending well. Cover and chill several hours to blend flavors. Serve on any green salad or with tomato salads.

Yield: Approximately 1⅔ cups.

Barbecue Sauces

Garlick maketh a man wynke, drynke, and stynke.

—Thomas Nashe, 15th Century

SWEET AND SOUR BARBECUE SAUCE

1 cup Spanish style
  tomato sauce
½ cup water
¼ cup cider vinegar
¼ cup finely chopped
  onion
2 teaspoons salt
1 teaspoon powdered
  mustard

1 clove garlic, crushed
⅛ teaspoon ground
  cayenne
2 tablespoons brown
  sugar
¼ cup fresh lemon
  juice
2 tablespoons butter or
  margarine

Combine all ingredients and cook slowly 5 minutes.
Use to barbecue chicken or turkey.

Yield: 2 cups.

FRESH LEMON BARBECUE SAUCE

¼ cup finely chopped
  onion
3 tablespoons salad oil
½ cup fresh lemon juice
⅓ cup vinegar
¼ cup ketchup
¼ cup water
1 tablespoon brown
  sugar

1¼ teaspoons salt
¼ teaspoon ground black
  pepper
1 clove garlic, crushed
1 teaspoon powdered
  mustard
¾ teaspoon ground red
  pepper

Sauté onion in salad oil until limp. Add remaining ingredients. Bring to boiling point. Cool.
Serve over steak, London broil, or roast beef.

Yield: 1½ cups.

PAPRIKA BARBECUE SAUCE

1 teaspoon powdered
  mustard
1 teaspoon water
⅔ cup fresh lemon juice
½ cup cider vinegar
⅓ cup ketchup
⅓ cup water
1½ tablespoons dark
  brown sugar
2 teaspoons paprika

1¼ teaspoons salt
¾ teaspoon ground red
  pepper
¼ cup finely chopped
  onion
1 clove garlic, crushed
⅛ teaspoon ground
  black pepper
4 tablespoons butter or
  margarine

Combine powdered mustard with water; let stand 10 minutes for flavor to develop. Then combine mustard with remaining ingredients. Boil 1 minute. Cool.

Excellent for chicken, pork, beef, or lamb. Will keep very well if stored in a covered jar in the refrigerator.

Yield: Approximately 2 cups.

DEVILED BARBECUE SAUCE

1 cup tomato juice
¼ cup cider vinegar
1 tablespoon instant
  minced onion
1 tablespoon brown
  sugar
1 teaspoon powdered
  mustard

1 teaspoon salt
¼ teaspoon whole allspice
¼ teaspoon ground black
  pepper
⅛ teaspoon cayenne
2 cloves garlic, crushed
1 tablespoon salad oil
1 beef bouillon cube

Combine all ingredients. Heat to boiling point.

Use as basting for barbecuing beef, lamb, veal, pork, and chicken. *Yield:* 1½ cups.

ALL-PURPOSE MILD
BARBECUE SAUCE

*1½ teaspoons powdered
  mustard
1 teaspoon chili powder
1 teaspoon onion salt
1 teaspoon celery salt
2 cloves garlic, crushed
1 bay leaf*

*2 tablespoons brown
  sugar
½ cup cider vinegar
2 cups tomato juice
½ cup ketchup
1 teaspoon red hot
  sauce*

Combine all ingredients in a saucepan. Simmer 5 minutes.
Use for swabbing onto and barbecuing all meats or poultry.

Yield: Approximately 3 cups.

WESTERN BARBECUE SAUCE

*1 cup butter or
  margarine
2½ cups water
¼ cup cider vinegar
1½ teaspoons powdered
  mustard
1 tablespoon salt
1 tablespoon sugar*

*½ cup finely chopped
  onion
1 teaspoon ground black
  pepper
1 teaspoon chili powder
4 cloves garlic, crushed
¼ teaspoon cayenne*

Combine all ingredients and simmer 30 minutes.
Pour over chicken or meat and soak 30 minutes before
cooking. Place on grill over a slow-burning charcoal fire.
Cook until done and outside has browned, basting as often
as meat or chicken looks dry. Cooking time depends upon
the heat of the fire.

Yield: 3¼ cups.

HOT BARBECUE SAUCE

½ cup fresh lemon juice
½ cup cider vinegar
⅓ cup ketchup
⅓ cup water
1 tablespoon brown
  sugar
1¼ teaspoons salt
1¼ teaspoons powdered
  mustard
1½ teaspoons paprika
¾ teaspoon ground black
  pepper

¼ teaspoon ground red
  pepper
1 teaspoon finely
  chopped onion
¼ teaspoon finely minced
  garlic
½ teaspoon red hot
  sauce
3 tablespoons butter or
  margarine

Combine all ingredients in a saucepan. Heat to boiling point.

Strain and use for barbecuing chicken, pork, beef, or lamb. This sauce will keep very well if stored in a covered jar in the refrigerator.

Yield: 2 cups.

THICK BARBECUE SAUCE

1 cup ketchup
⅓ cup cider vinegar
½ cup water
2 tablespoons brown
  sugar
¼ cup finely chopped
  onion
2 tablespoons fresh
  lemon juice

½ teaspoon salt
1 teaspoon powdered
  mustard
½ teaspoon ground
  black pepper
2 cloves garlic, crushed
¼ teaspoon cayenne

Combine all ingredients in a saucepan. Cover and cook 5 minutes.

Use to barbecue spareribs, pork chops, veal chops, or chicken.

Yield: About 1¾ cups.

HALIBUT MARINADE

¼ cup lemon juice
½ cup salad oil
4 cloves garlic, crushed
½ teaspoon salt
½ teaspoon black pepper
  or 7 peppercorns

½ teaspoon
  Worcestershire sauce
1 tablespoon ketchup
⅛ teaspoon ground bay
  leaf

Combine all ingredients and mix well. Pour over 2 pounds halibut steak. Marinate 6 to 8 hours, turning occasionally.

Broil halibut for 10 to 15 minutes on each side, or until tender and browned. While broiling, baste with remaining sauce.

This marinade may also be used on other fish and meats—lamb chops, pork chops, and steaks.

Yield: 6 generous servings.

HICKORY LEMON BASTING SAUCE

1⅓ cups fresh lemon
  juice
2¼ cups olive or salad
  oil

4 teaspoons chili powder
3 tablespoons hickory
  salt
2 cloves garlic, crushed

Blend ingredients for sauce; let stand 2 hours or overnight in refrigerator. For chicken, baste frequently with sauce while broiling. Allow 20 to 30 minutes on each side. Remaining sauce may be stored in refrigerator.

Yield: 1 quart, or enough for 30 to 40 broiler halves.

GOURMET BASTING SAUCE

1½ cups fresh lemon juice

1½ cups olive or salad oil

2 tablespoons ground marjoram

½ teaspoon freshly ground peppercorns

2 tablespoons salt

1 cup Worcestershire sauce

2 cloves garlic, crushed

Blend together all ingredients for sauce. Let stand several hours or overnight in refrigerator. Brush steaks or chops frequently with sauce while broiling or frying. Remaining sauce may be stored in refrigerator.

Yield: 1 quart, or enough for 30 to 40 steaks.

MARINADE FOR LAMB OR BEEF

2 cups fresh lemon juice

2 tablespoons grated lemon peel

2 cups salad oil

2 teaspoons salt

½ teaspoon freshly ground pepper

½ teaspoon ground savory

1 teaspoon ground oregano

3 tablespoons brown sugar

½ cup minced onion

1 tablespoon chopped parsley

1 or 2 cloves garlic, crushed

Combine all ingredients and marinate lamb or beef pieces several hours or overnight in refrigerator. *Yield:* 1 quart.

Sauces

Garlic Retards Early Aging and Rising Blood Pressure.

—Early American newspaper advertisement

BAGNA CAUDA

1 pound butter
4 large cloves garlic
16 anchovy fillets,
    minced
2 cups heavy cream

Selection of: crisp
    endive, celery, green
    pepper strips,
    cucumber strips, bread
    sticks or toasted
    Italian bread

Melt butter in skillet, being sure not to brown. Add whole garlic cloves and sauté slowly about 10 minutes, making certain not to brown garlic or butter. Add anchovies, mixing until well blended. Slowly add cream, stirring constantly. Remove garlic cloves. Keep sauce hot on a warming tray or in a chafing dish. Use as a dip for selection of cold vegetables, bread sticks, and toast.

Yield: Approximately 4 cups.

AIOLI SAUCE

8 cloves garlic, crushed
¼ teaspoon salt
2 egg yolks

1 cup olive oil
Juice of ½ lemon

Cream together garlic, salt, and egg yolks. Add oil a few drops at a time, beating vigorously until two tablespoons of oil have been added. Add remaining oil slowly, beating vigorously as oil is added. Slowly add lemon juice. Beat vigorously. Serve with hot or cold fish.

Yield: 1½ cups.

MARINARA SAUCE

1 clove garlic, finely
  chopped
½ cup chopped onion
¼ cup olive oil
4 cups canned Italian
  tomatoes

½ teaspoon oregano
½ cup chopped parsley
1 tablespoon chopped
  basil leaves
Salt and pepper to
  taste

Sauté garlic and onion in oil until browned. Add remaining ingredients and simmer uncovered until thickened, about 1 hour.

Yield: 3 cups.

ITALIAN SWEET SAUSAGE SAUCE

1½ pounds Italian sweet
  sausage meat
1 teaspoon salt
1 8-ounce can tomato
  paste
3½ cups (1 pound 13
  ounces) canned
  tomatoes

1 clove garlic, crushed
1 tablespoon instant
  minced onion
1 teaspoon oregano
  leaves
1 teaspoon sugar
⅛ teaspoon ground
  black pepper

Cut sausage into ¼-inch slices and brown. Drain off fat. Add salt, tomato paste, tomatoes, garlic, and onion. Bring to boiling point and simmer, uncovered, 45 minutes. Add oregano, sugar, and ground black pepper 10 minutes before cooking time is up. Use as a sauce for spaghetti, cooked rice, or mashed potatoes.

Yield: 5¼ cups.

PIZZAIOLA SAUCE

2 tablespoons olive or
   salad oil
2½ cups tomatoes
2 tablespoons tomato
   paste
1 teaspoon salt

½ teaspoon oregano
   leaves, crumbled
1 teaspoon parsley flakes
¼ teaspoon ground
   black pepper
2 cloves garlic, crushed

Heat oil in a skillet. Add remaining ingredients and cook 20 to 30 minutes, or until medium thick. Serve over fish, chops, or steak.

Yield: 2½ cups.

PESTO ALLA GENOVESE

(Basil and Garlic Sauce)

2 cloves garlic, chopped
3 tablespoons minced
   fresh basil leaves
3 tablespoons grated
   imported Parmesan cheese

1 tablespoon grated
   Romano cheese
1 tablespoon chopped
   pine nuts
½ teaspoon salt
6 tablespoons olive oil

Combine all ingredients except olive oil in a mortar. Pound with a pestle to blend to a smooth paste, gradually adding olive oil, until a smooth sauce is made. (Or use an electric blender.)

Pesto is used as a sauce for spaghetti mixed with about 2 tablespoons butter, and served with grated Parmesan cheese. This recipe makes enough sauce for 1 pound of spaghetti. (A spoonful of pesto may be added to hot minestrone or ravioli dishes for piquant flavoring.)

PROVENCALE SAUCE

2 1-pound 13-ounce
   cans tomatoes
½ cup olive oil
1 teaspoon salt
¼ teaspoon freshly
   ground black pepper

1 teaspoon sugar
2 cloves garlic, crushed
1 tablespoon chopped
   parsley

Drain tomatoes and chop.
Heat olive oil in a heavy saucepan. Add tomatoes and remaining ingredients. Cover and simmer 30 minutes.

Yield: Approximately 2 cups.

GARLIC CLAM SAUCE

2 tablespoons olive oil
½ teaspoon garlic salt
½ teaspoon crushed basil
   leaves
¼ teaspoon crushed
   oregano leaves

1 teaspoon parsley flakes
1 teaspoon capers
1 7½-ounce can minced
   clams, drained
½ cup sour cream

Heat together first 6 ingredients for 5 minutes. Stir in can of drained minced clams. Heat about 3 minutes. Cool. Stir in sour cream. Store in refrigerator to use as an appetizer dip or on top of boiled or broiled fish steaks. Or heat and use on veal scallopini or cooked spaghetti.

Yield: 1 cup.

INDEX